How to Grow Your Church

Daniel King

I dedicate this book to Billy Joe Daugherty,
a pastor who was dedicated to reaching out to his community
and the world with every available evangelistic method.

Thanks to Luke Inberg and Jessica King
for helping to edit and proof-read this book.

How to Grow Your Church

ISBN: 1-931810-18-4

Copyright: 2015

Daniel King - King Ministries International
PO Box 701113
Tulsa, OK 74170 USA
1-877-431-4276
daniel@kingministries.com
www.kingministries.com

Table of Contents

Section 4: Sharing Your Faith   43

Outreach Idea #79: Tracts
Outreach Idea #80: Baptism Service
Outreach Idea #81: Baby Dedications
Outreach Idea #82: "Cell"-vation Service

Section 5: Meet a Need   55

Outreach Idea #83: Car Wash
Outreach Idea #84: Clothing Drive
Outreach Idea #85: Yard Sale
Outreach Idea #86: Food Ministry
Outreach Idea #87: Nursing Home Outreach
Outreach Idea #88: Rehabilitation House
Outreach Idea #89: Dream Center
Outreach Idea #90: Give an Abused Person a Home to Live In
Outreach Idea #91: Prayer Call Center
Outreach Idea #92: Adopt-A-Block
Outreach Idea #93: Pick Up Trash
Outreach Idea #94: Light up the World
Outreach Idea #95: Pet Adoption Day
Outreach Idea #96: Seminars
Outreach Idea #97: Host a Financial Skills Seminar

Section 6: Be Social   63

Outreach Idea #98: Appreciation Meals for Law Enforcement
Outreach Idea #99: Take Business Men and Women out for Lunch
Outreach Idea #100: Host a Block Party
Outreach Idea #101: Cooking Classes
Outreach Idea #102: Circus Family Night
Outreach Idea #103: Visiting Homes
Outreach Idea #104: Go Where the Sinners Are
Outreach Idea #105: Host a Sporting Event
Outreach Idea #106: Family Movie Day
Outreach Idea #107: Church Carnival

What is Your Best Outreach Idea?

Introduction

Dear Pastor,

Do you want your church to grow? What is your church doing to reach out to the lost? Are your members excited about sharing their faith with their family, friends, and co-workers?

What happens when a soccer team scores a goal? The spectator stands erupt. People jump to their feet, clap, shout, and cheer. When is the one time that heaven acts this way? Jesus said, *"...There is joy in the presence of the angels of God over one sinner who repents"* (Luke 15:10 NKJV). Heaven celebrates when a sinner gets saved. The way the church scores goals is by leading people to Jesus. How many goals is your church scoring? This book will help your church score more heavenly goals!

In this book, you will find ideas from around the world that will help your church grow. Contained in these pages are over one hundred and fifty innovative ideas on how your local church can be involved in reaching out to your community. Each one of these ideas has been successful somewhere. They are tried, tested, and proven to work.

There are two mistakes you could make after reading this book. The

first is to try none of the ideas in this book. The second mistake is to try to implement every idea in this book—if you tried to do that, you would quickly overwhelm your congregation.

Marilyn Hickey says, "Ask God to give you the key to reaching each place that you work in." The evangelism techniques that work in one nation do not necessarily work in other nations. In Ethiopia, people are attracted to our Gospel Festival by the thousands because of miracles. In Indonesia, we attract young people by using music in a concert setting. In Sudan, many people come because of the food given away. So the question is: What is the best way for you to catch the attention of people in your area?

Treat this book like a buffet menu: pick and choose the outreach ideas that work best for you and adapt them to the context of your church. As you step out in faith, watch: your church members will become more excited about evangelism, your church will grow as you reach out to more people, and your community will be impacted by the Good News of salvation in Jesus Christ.

Becoming an Evangelistic Church

I am an evangelist. I have never been a pastor, but I have worked with hundreds of pastors in North America and trained thousands of pastors around the world to impact their communities with the Gospel. If the pastor is like a shepherd, the evangelist is like the sheepdog who runs around and gathers up the lost sheep. We should work together to reach the lost. I am passionate about evangelism, and I think every church should be excited about telling people about Jesus.

As an evangelist, I have two roles. My first job is to lead people to Jesus. In this, I have been successful. By doing massive miracle crusades, I had the opportunity to lead over 1,000,000 people in a salvation prayer before the age of thirty. My second role as an evangelist is to equip believers for evangelism. According to Ephesians 4:11, the five-fold ministry gifts are given for *"the equipping of the saints for the work of the ministry."* In order for the Church to truly grow, every believer needs to be sharing his or her faith. Paul told Timothy to *"Do the work of the evangelist"* (2 Timothy 4:5). This instruction is for every believer.

Unfortunately, the word "evangelism" has acquired some negative connotations. Greg Fraser says, "One thing churches and the world

agree on is that they both hate evangelism." Often when people hear the word "evangelist" they imagine a television personality with slicked-back hair pleading for money, or a man on a street corner with a big sign yelling at people through a megaphone. So, when the typical churchgoer hears that he should "evangelize," he suddenly sees a mental image of himself trying to push religion down someone's throat. While such images are vivid, nothing could be farther from the truth. To me, evangelism is simply anything a church does to attract and influence people to get connected with God.

What is an evangelistic church?

The word "evangelist" comes from the Greek word *euangelistes*. The root word for *euangelistes* is *euangelion*--which is translated as "gospel." Both these words are derived from the word *angelos*, meaning "angel" or "messenger." The *angelos* type of messenger is one who brings tidings of a great victory or good news. So, in ancient Greece when a battle was won, a messenger (evangelist) would be sent to all the surrounding cities to announce the victory. The word "gospel" means good news, and the evangelist is one who preaches the good news.

The word "evangelist" is used three times in the New Testament. Philip is called an evangelist (Acts 21:8); Paul mentions evangelists in his list of ministry offices, along with apostles, prophets, pastors, and teachers (Ephesians 4:11); and Paul tells Timothy to do the *"work of an evangelist"* (2 Timothy 4:5). (The fact that the word evangelist is only used three times is not meant to demean the office of the evangelist. The title of bishop is also used three times. Deacon is only found twice. Amazingly, given the current prominence in the body of Christ on the local church pastor, the word pastor only occurs once.) However, the root word of evangelist (*euangelion*, the Greek word for "gospel") is used 74 times in the New Testament and the verb form *euangelizomai* is used an additional 52 times.

* Jesus is the first Evangelist of the New Testament since He went about "preaching the good news [*euangelion*] of the kingdom" (Matt. 4:23).

* Throughout the writings of Paul, who used *euangelion* 60 times, the heart of the Gospel message is that God provided for the salvation of humankind through the birth, death, and resurrection of Jesus.

* The angel who announced Jesus' birth was an evangelist because he proclaimed *"good news that will cause great joy for all the people"* (Luke 2:10 NIV).

* The early Church was full of evangelists because they *"preached the word wherever they went"* (Acts 8:4 NIV).

The evangelistic gift is one of the five-fold ministry gifts (Ephesians 4:11), and this evangelistic gift is needed in the Body of Christ today. The evangelistic church is equally needed, doing mass-evangelism and one-on-one evangelism (Acts 8:5-8; 26-39). In addition to being directly involved in soul winning, the evangelistic church is called to train their members to be soul winners (Ephesians 4:12).

The evangelistic church:
* Leads the lost to Christ.
* Equips the saints for evangelism.
* Reaches out to both individuals and multitudes.
* Preaches the simple Gospel, not the latest, greatest, brand-new flavor of the week.
* Witnesses signs and wonders following the preaching of the Word.
* Is a shining light in the midst of a dark world.
* Is like a spiritual obstetrician who gives birth to new believers.
* Is the advertising agency for God's kingdom.
* Is like elite Navy Seals who are the first to head into enemy territory.
* Is like shock troops on the frontlines of the battle for lost souls.

* Is like a farmer who focuses on plowing ground, sowing seed, and reaping a harvest.

Church Growth

Ultimately, church growth is in the hands of God. The Holy Spirit prepares people's hearts; the Father draws them close; and Jesus saves them from their sins. But in addition to the divine element in salvation, there are many practical things the church can do to reach people. *"How then shall they call on Him in whom they have not believed? And how shall they believe in Him of whom they have not heard? And how shall they hear without a preacher?"* (Romans 10:14 NKJV).

In some ways churches are a lot like businesses. A dealership may not sell a Cadillac to everyone who comes in the door, but they won't sell a Cadillac to anyone who does not come in the door. So the secret to church growth is getting people in the door on a regular basis.

Imagine a funnel. At the top it is wide and at the bottom it is narrow. Your evangelism program is the top of your funnel. You want to put as many people in the top of your funnel as you possibly can. The more people hear about your church, the more people will visit your church; the more people attend your church, the more people will be saved and become disciples of Jesus at your church. Not everyone at the top of the funnel who hears the Gospel will become a disciple, but the bigger the top of your funnel is, the more people will come out the bottom of your funnel.

Evangelism is God's marketing system. Coca-Cola has done a magnificent job of advertising their brand, spending tens of thousands of dollars every day to do so. They spend over three million dollars for a 30-second advertisement during the Super Bowl. In every Central American country, the walls are plastered with signs urging the

thirsty to drink Coca-Cola. At a store in the middle of Africa, hours from a paved road, I saw a tin sign with their logo.

Marketing studies show that the typical person needs seven positive exposures to a new product before they are ready to purchase it. This is why companies like Coca-Cola spend millions of dollars on advertising. Evangelism is the marketing department of the local church. If you want your church to grow, you must give the members of your church opportunities to positively "market" your church to the community.

If you fail to plan, you plan to fail.

Evangelism does not happen by accident. Your church needs a detailed, thought-out strategy for evangelism. This plan should have two distinct systems. The first is an evangelism system (a systematic plan for reaching new people). The second is an assimilation system (a systematic plan for turning converts into disciples). These systems can be developed by asking the right questions. While the answer to these questions is going to be different for every church, it is vital that you and your church ask the questions.

First, develop an Evangelism System.
What is your plan for church growth?
How will you reach out to your community?
How often do you preach on evangelism?
Does your church give your members opportunities to help reach people?
Have you developed any tools (tracts, door hangers, t-shirts, etc.) that can be used to lead people to Jesus?
How do you get new people in the door of your church?
How do you develop relationships with new people?
How do you invite new people?
How do you attract new visitors?
Do you have an advertising budget and plan?

If a new family visits your church, do you give them an opportunity to get saved?

Do you clearly present the Gospel at least once in every service?

How many events each year does your church do that are specifically focused on evangelism?

Second, develop an Assimilation System. This is your discipleship program. When Jesus made us fishers of men, He was not thinking about "catch and release." Instead we are called to "catch and teach." When visitors walk in the front doors of your church, how do you identify them, welcome them, capture their information, and follow-up on them? How do you keep the people you have? How do you close the "back door" of your church? How do you get a visitor to come back a second time? How do you turn a seeker into a disciple? How do you follow-up on the people that visit your church? How do you turn converts into disciples?

Communicate your vision for soul winning.

Asking the right questions will help you formulate your plan for evangelism and for discipleship, But to become an evangelistic church you will need to do more than have a plan—you will need to share it too. You have heard it quoted a million times, "Without vision, the people perish," but pastors should realize, "Without vision, the people go to another parish." Do you communicate your vision regularly? People need to hear your vision 1,000 times before they know it. If your newest nursery worker cannot recite the church vision at a moment's notice, you have not communicated it enough. So, communicate your vision: let people know why your church exists and why they are a part of it; let them know where your church is going and what it is becoming; let them know the importance of being an evangelistic church. As you communicate your vision and plan for evangelism, you are empowering your church members to do the work of an evangelist.

Section 1:
Growing Your Church

Outreach Idea #1: Ask Your Members to Invite People to Church. Statistics show that 80% of people who are personally invited to church are willing to visit. Unfortunately, as Bill Bright said in his book "The Coming Revival," only 2% of those who go to church ever invite someone to go with them to church. The gap between these two statistics is the reason why many churches are not growing.

Outreach Idea #2: Each One Reach One. For this outreach, the pastor challenges each member of the congregation to bring at least one unsaved person to church on a particular Sunday. On that day the entire service is geared towards communicating the Gospel with those who have never heard it before.

Outreach Idea #3: Invest in Your Children's Ministry. Mark Rutland says, "You can't grow a church long-term by focusing on youth ministry, but you can by focusing on kid's ministry." What is Mark's reasoning behind this comment? Well, while we do want to reach out to youth, even if your youth ministry doubles in size, it's less likely that their parents will come to church. However, if your children's ministry on Sunday morning doubles in size, it is very likely that the kid's parents or guardians are sitting in your adult service as

well. And it is likely that your offerings will be significantly bigger.

It is vital for your children's ministry to be safe, professional, and high class. When parents of young children buy a vehicle, they make their purchase decisions based on the needs of their children. A single man might buy a muscle car, but a family usually buys a mini-van. When families go shopping for a church, the look of the children's ministry often makes or breaks their decision.

At one church I was preaching at, my wife Jessica went to drop our children off in the nursery. The nursery worker had stepped out of the nursery to go to the bathroom leaving three toddlers to play by themselves. In the corner of the nursery there was a pile of junk including some building supplies with nails sticking out of a piece of wood. Insulation hung out of the ceiling. Needless to say, my wife did not leave our children in that nursery. If I had been a visitor and seen that situation, I would have turned around and walked out of the church before the service even began.

Mark Rutland says that in a healthy church, your youth group should be about 10% of your Sunday morning attendance and your children's ministry should be about 20%.

Outreach Idea #4: Youth Ministry. Christianity is always one generation away from extinction. If the church does not reach the youth, then the church will quickly become obsolete. Today's youth do not want to be spectators, they want to be participators. Do not expect youth to just sit in pews while you preach to them. Put their energy to work and ask them to help make a difference in the lives of others. Turn your young people into soul winners and allow them to use their talents for God. Perhaps your young people could start one of these teams:
* Dance Team

* Drama Team
* Mime Team
* Clown Team
* Puppet Team
* Flag Twirling Team
* Face Painting Team

Outreach Idea #5: Start a Saturday Night Service. In the hustle and bustle of modern living, the church must offer more options to the busy consumer. Some people simply do not wish to come or are unable to come to church on Sunday morning. By making a service available at another time, you will attract a whole different group of people.

Outreach Idea #6: Start a Sunday School. Many churches no longer have Sunday School, but fifty years ago Sunday School was the backbone of the church. It can still be a valuable tool for both discipleship and church growth.

When Mark Rutland was invited to pastor Calvary Assembly in Orlando, Florida, the church was in serious trouble. They had a five thousand-seat auditorium with only nine hundred people sitting in the seats. They owed over 15 million dollars on their building and just their debt maintenance cost $125,000 every month. Rutland knew that he needed to put a hip in every seat and that every hip needed to have a wallet. The tool he decided to use was Sunday School.

He promoted his singles pastor (an enthusiastic ex-con) to become the Christian Education Director. They started promoting Sunday School classes to the entire church.

The ushers and greeters said they did not have enough time to go

to Sunday School and then to put on their official jackets. So Rutland started a Sunday School class just for the Ushers and Greeters and it became a requirement for those who wanted to be ushers and greeter.

Rutland had a choir Sunday School class that was mandatory for the choir and another mandatory class for small group leaders. He had one group for lawyers and another for doctors and another for blue-collar workers. He used every trick in the book to get people to attend his Sunday School classes. Rutland jokingly says, "When vision and leadership don't work, use guilt and manipulation." He encouraged the different Sunday School classes to compete for attendance and participation prizes.

In two years, his Sunday School went from zero participation to the largest Sunday school in the Assemblies of God in Florida with over 1,500 people participating. When Rutland left the church, 3,700 people attended the morning service.

Outreach Idea #7: Altar Calls. Give people an opportunity to receive Jesus in every service. From the time I was a young child I attended services at Victory Christian Center in Tulsa, Oklahoma. Not once did I ever attend a service where Pastor Billy Joe Daugherty did not give an altar call. His church was always reaching people because he had a heart for evangelism.

Outreach Idea #8: Visitor Follow-Up. It is important to close the "back door" of your church. Once people visit your church, how do you get them to come back for a second visit? Mark Rutland developed a system he called DARE: Direct Access Relational Evangelism. This is how it worked at his church:
1. Ask visitors to give you their name, address, phone number, and e-mail. You can offer a little gift in exchange for this information or

ask them to drop the info card in the offering bucket.

2. Give the card to your phone team. These can be elderly members of your congregation who enjoy talking on the phone. The phone team can call visitors on Sunday afternoon to thank them for coming to the church.

3. Pass the card to a small group leader who lives in the visitor's part of town. She should call the visitor on Monday and invite them to visit the small group. This way the visitor would receive two personal phone calls within twenty-four hours of visiting the church.

4. Add the info to the church's database and e-mail list. Advertise special events to everyone who has ever visited the church.

Outreach Idea #9: Cell Groups / Bible Studies in Homes and Businesses / G-12 Groups. David Yonggi Cho pastors the world's largest church in South Korea. He uses cell groups to disciple his congregation. He originally started the cell groups so that his church would survive in case North Korea ever attacked. Even in a big church, people can have a personal connection by participating in a small group.

Calvary Christian Center in Sacramento, California, has implemented the G-12 system (developed by Cesar Castellanos in Columbia). Every person in the church is mentored in a group of twelve (because Jesus had twelve disciples). The system has four steps:

1. Win: Evangelism aims to win people to a new belief in Christ.

2. Consolidate: This stage involves attending an Encounter with God weekend retreat, where a new believer is "consolidated" in the faith by prayer, exposing of generational curses, casting out of demons and deep repentance.

3. Disciple: At this stage, individuals are enrolled in the School of Leaders, which will begin to train the believer to recruit new disciples.

4. Send: Leaders are sent out to do the work by establishing a new cell group.

Outreach Idea #10: Take Christian Lingo Out of Your Songs, Witnessing, and Preaching. "Christian lingo" is any word that is likely to confuse a visitor. Choosing not to use Christian lingo is not a decision to water down the gospel message. It is, in fact, a way of making the good news available to people who do not understand the specialized language a regular church member is used to. So in trying to reach out, do not use lots of religious words that are confusing to the unsaved. For example, "washed in the Blood" sounds like something a vampire would say and no one knows what "bringing in the sheaves" means. Update your language so ordinary people can understand what you are saying.

Outreach Idea #11: Give Your Church a Face-Lift. Mark Rutland says the best value for your church growth dollar is improving the look of your church property. When a visitor enters your church property, what do they see? Do they see weeds around your church sign? Do they see peeling paint and missing shingles on the roof? Does the nursery look clean? Are the wastebaskets in the washroom overflowing? Are there outdated bulletins strewn across the table by the front door? Are the plastic plants on the stage caked in dust? Are signs posted that clearly communicate where to park, where to take your children, and where the washrooms are located?
Walk through your church and look at it through the eyes of a first-time visitor. Does your church look clean, comfortable, and inviting? Is it decorated to attract the type of person you want to attend your church?

To increase the perceived value of your church, invest in landscaping, paint, new tile in the bathrooms, attractive signage, and a regular cleaning service. You never have a second chance to make a good first impression.

Outreach Idea #12: Involve the Lead Pastor. The church reflects

who the pastor is. Many pastors make the mistake of appointing an evangelism director to handle church outreaches and then never showing up themselves to participate. The pastor wonders why the evangelism director is unable to generate much enthusiasm or participation. The anointing flows down from the head. When the pas- tor participates, the congregation will participate. People will not do what the pastor says; they will do what the pastor does. If outreach is highlighted and preached on from the platform, the vision to be involved will be imparted to the congregation.

Outreach Idea #13: Affiliate Visitor Commission Plan. Kaylisa Ferguson from the Bahamas describes a program her church uses to encourage church members to invite friends. She says, "What do you do when your church members become apathetic about inviting people to church? How can you motivate them to partner with you to bring the lost to church?" Kaylisa's answer to that question? "Well, you pay them."

"The purpose of the Affiliate Visitor Commission Plan is to reward the member that brings the most new visitors to church during a given month (not including children). In the business world, if you are an affiliate for Amazon.com and you sell their products, you receive a commission on the volume that you sell. This plan has the same intent: Members are paid an earthly commission for bringing new visitors to the church where they have the opportunity to meet God.

"The church board in the Bahamas decided to give $180 each month to the winning member. Because of the prize, church members are motivated to ask several persons during the month instead of just one or two people.

"This is how the plan works. When a visitor comes to the service, there is a guestbook that he/she signs giving their name, address, age

range, telephone number and the person who invited them. This log is kept for the entire month. If your church has visitor cards, these can be used instead of the guestbook. The entries are totaled by member name to produce a winner. On the first Sunday of the next month, the pastor announces the amount of visitors for the previous month and the winner. After service, the member can pick up his or her check. If there is a tie, this is also announced and the money is split between the winners. This has produced effective growth in our church's membership as people join our local church through this method."

If you are having difficulty motivating your congregation to invite the unsaved to your church, perhaps Kaylisa's idea might help to change that!

Section 2:
Advertise to Evangelize

Outreach Idea #14: Advertising. Once an advertising executive was asked how much of his million-dollar advertising budget was effective. He replied, "Only half of my advertising produces any results." The follow-up question came, "If only half of your advertising is effective, why do you spend the full million? Why don't you cut your budget in half?" The executive explained, "The problem is we do not know which half of our advertising is the effective half."

Many churches make the mistake of doing a half-hearted advertising campaign and then dropping it when it does not immediately seem to produce results. However, advertising is not something that will always produce instant results. The best advertising campaigns put together a strategic, long-term plan.

The average consumer needs to be exposed to a product seven times before they are willing to give the new product a try. Church advertising must be visible over a long period of time in order to start producing regular results.

Outreach Idea #15: Billboards. Try renting a billboard in an area near your church with lots of traffic.

Outreach Idea #16: Newspaper Ads. Whenever you are doing a special service, run an ad in the local newspaper.

Outreach Idea #17: The Yellow Pages. Many people who move to a new city look in the phone book in order to find a church. If your church is prominently displayed, you will have more visitors.

Outreach Idea #18: TV Advertising. Rather than spend your money on one half-hour program once a week, spend your budget on thirty 30-second spots.

Outreach Idea #19: Radio Advertising. If you advertise on a Christian radio station you are not really evangelizing because non-believers for the most part do not listen to Christian radio. Instead, try advertising during the six o'clock news on the most popular radio station in your city.

Outreach Idea #20: Coupon Book. The Father's House in Morinville, Canada, advertises in local coupon books. For them, this is less expensive than reaching the same number of homes via a newspaper advertisement. Perhaps you could include a coupon for a free coffee on Sunday morning or a free book or CD at your church bookstore.

Outreach Idea #21: Postcards. Imagine hand-delivering an invitation to a special service at your church to every house within a three-mile radius of your church. How long would it take you to do that? Now, imagine if you could pay someone to do all that work for you. How much do you think it would cost? For about $0.40 apiece you can print and mail a postcard via the national postal service to every house in your neighborhood. Make your postcards big, colorful, and easy to read. You have about two seconds to catch someone's attention before they throw your postcard in the trash. But, the good news is that a postcard is far more likely to be read than a letter.

Outreach Idea #22: Turn Your Church Members into Walking Billboards. Here are some ideas for how your church members can help you preach the Gospel without ever opening their mouths.
1. Church bumper stickers
2. Church t-shirts
3. Church hats
4. Church business cards
5. Door hangers
6. Church tracts
7. Invitations to your church for special events

Outreach Idea #23: Send Out a Press Release Every Time You do an Event. Call your local newspaper and ask for the contact information for the editor. Every time you do a special event or service at your church, send out a press release. A news story about your church is far more valuable than paid advertising. When you pay for advertising, you talk about yourself. But in a news story someone else talks about you which gives the story added credibility.

Outreach Idea #24: Ask Your Local Television Station to do a Story on Your Church. Call your local news station and invite a reporter to come interview you. On a slow news day, a feel-good story about how a local church is loving people in the community may be just what a reporter is looking for.

Outreach Idea #25: Television (Tell-A-Vision). If you are a small to medium-sized local church, do not try to go on national television. You will just waste your money. The most effective use of your money is to focus your program on your local market. Television can be very expensive and because there are so many channels, it is easy to get lost in the clutter. However, according to Phil Cooke (author of "The Last TV Evangelist"), if television is done correctly (with good production values and creative content) it can still be

useful for reaching people with the Gospel.

When Mark Rutland pastored Calvary Assembly in Orlando, one-third of his visitors came because they saw him preaching on television. When he took over the church, it was in massive debt, but when he was going over the accounts, he noticed the previous pastor had pre-paid for several months of airtime. Rutland negotiated with the station to use part of the pre-paid airtime to pay for production and went on TV for free. From this experience, Rutland says he learned, "Do not focus on your lack, focus on what you have."

Outreach Idea #26: Social Media. Perhaps the best bang for your advertising buck will be on social media which is often completely free. Every church should have a social media volunteer who sits in the back of the church with a laptop. This volunteer should tweet on Twitter and post on Facebook the best sermon points as the pastor preaches. A great tool to use is Hootsuite.com. Encourage your congregation to post on social media sites during the worship service. This will expand the number of people who are blessed by the message.

Outreach Idea #27: Facebook. Chris Forbes wrote "Facebook for Pastors," a great e-book that is available online for free. He says, "Facebook is a community of people who need ministry, crave real relationships, and need the influence of the gospel and spiritual guidance from pastors." Facebook is designed to be a network of like-minded people. You will find that most of your church members are on Facebook. As you find friends on Facebook, you will start to get to know them better and discover many opportunities to minister to them.

1. Go to Facebook.com and sign up for a free profile.
2. Add a profile photo to your account.
3. Post frequent status updates.

4. Comment on and "like" other people's status updates.

5. Post videos and links to content that you find interesting.

6. Create a group for your church or ministry.

Outreach Idea #28: Facebook Events. Elizabeth J. Foster suggests setting up an event on Facebook to encourage church members to invite people to church on a particular Sunday.

1. To make an event on Facebook, click on the link that says "Events."

2. Click on "Add a new event."

3. Describe the event with words like this: "Hey guys, I've been praying, and God has really been putting it on my heart to invite the people I know who are around me who are not saved to church and really just love on them and show them that God cares for them and that He sent His only Son, Jesus, to die on the cross for them, So I put this little group together in order to invite all of you guys to join me in this outreach. If you would be interested in joining me in this, invite your friends, coworkers and the people you know that are not saved on DATE at TIME to CHURCH NAME."

4. Invite your church, Bible study, connect group or even just your Christian friends who would be interested in participating.

Outreach Idea #29: Twitter. Can you communicate deep eternal truths about God in 140 characters or less? Then Twitter.com is for you.

Outreach Idea #30: YouTube. Last year I asked God, "What is the key for us to reach people in our culture?" I felt God say, "Turn the internet into a fishing net for lost souls." So I recorded a simple five-minute video on "How Can I be Saved?" and posted the video on YouTube.com, a website that allows anyone to post a video and share it. The results have been phenomenal. In the past twelve months, 69,502 people have watched the video. On average, 133 people have watched the video every day it has been available. Google, the popu-

lar Internet browser, recommends our video for anyone who types in the question "How can I be saved?" People have watched the video from the United States, Canada, England, Australia, South Africa, India and many other countries. Over 400 people have posted the video on their Facebook page for their friends to watch.

Thousands of unsaved people have now watched the video on "How Can I Be Saved?" The reason I know they are not saved is because of the comments they make. Here are a few:

* A YouTube user going by the name *eternalcrumpet* wrote, "what a load of delusional B.S."
* *MasterAtheistic* says, "2 seconds in and I want to smash that stupid, smug grin off his stupid fatuous face!"
* *Shwah7* complained, "This is the first result when searching for "Atheism" good job YouTube."
* *Boldziga* says, "LOLLOOLOLOLOL im atheist ;D"

Over 700 comments have been made and many of them are full of profanity, hate, and sinfulness. But the comments do not bother me. Why? Because in the middle of writing these comments, people who desperately need Jesus are watching the video! Lives are being impacted by the Gospel.

* For example, recently *Ps3scaryNinja* typed: "...God please forgive me for my sins."

In order to lead people to Jesus, we have to go where they are. There are many people who would never dream of visiting a church, but they will watch an internet video on their laptop.

Section 3:
An Outreach for
Every Season

Outreach Idea #31: Use the Calendar. At the beginning of the year, the church should pull out a calendar and choose specific dates for doing community outreaches. Every church should do at least four major outreaches each year. These should be spread out so that the church has one evangelistic opportunity every quarter. For example, one church in Dallas, Texas plans a special outreach every Easter, Independence Day, Back-to-School, and at Christmas.

These outreaches give church members an outlet for evangelism. They serve as training ground for empowering believers on how to share their faith.

January
Outreach Idea #32: New Year's Day - January 1. Host a "New Start" event at your church on the first day of the year. Help people set New Year's resolutions.

Outreach Idea #33: Fast and Pray Together as a Church. Every year, Christ for the Nations Church in Dallas, Texas, does a corporate fast for the first twenty-one days of the new year. During this time they specifically pray for people to be saved. Some people fast one meal, others eat only fruit and vegetables, others drink nothing

but water for the full twenty-one days, but everyone in the church participates in some way. This brings amazing unity to the church and the fast bears fruit throughout the year.

Prayer and evangelism go hand in hand. If you pray and never evangelize, no one will ever get saved, but evangelizing without praying is just as bad. It's like walking. Prayer is the first step, and then evangelism is the second step. Prayer. Evangelism. Prayer. Evangelism. Step-by-step you walk with God.

February

Outreach Idea #34: Black History Month. Use Black History Month as an opportunity to reach out to the African-American community. Each week during February you can celebrate the life of a different hero like Rosa Parks, Martin Luther King, Jr. or George Washington Carver.

Outreach Idea #35: Super Bowl Sunday. The sports fanatics in your church want to watch the big game. Do not schedule a mandatory prayer meeting while the Super Bowl airs or you will end up forcing all your elders to choose between staying in your church or missing the most popular sporting event of the year. Instead, why not use the event as an opportunity for your men to invite unbelievers to come to church? Invite people to come watch the game on the big screen in the auditorium. Provide lots of snacks. Give an altar call during the half-time show.

Outreach Idea #36: Valentine's Day Banquet. Job Ozovehe recommends preparing a beautiful banquet for couples on the most romantic day of the year. The banquet can take place at the church or in a neutral place like a five-star hotel. A month before the event, encourage couples in the church to befriend an unchurched couple and give them a free ticket to the event. Here are some ideas for

making the event a success:
* Have a slow-dancing competition and give a prize to the best couple.
* Play a game to see who really knows their partner.
* Ask each person to write a paragraph about the most memorable day of their marriage.
* Ask each couple to make a list of his or her spouse's best attributes.
* Give a prize for the most romantic poem.

Ask three couples from your church to share how they have experienced the power of God's love in their marriages. At the end, share the Gospel, and focus on the impact of salvation on marriages. Give an opportunity for people to get saved.

March
Outreach Idea #37: March Madness. Matt Sampson from Alberta, Canada, does basketball outreaches during the college basketball playoffs. He invites teenagers from the community to a gym and sponsors a basketball tournament. During the event he builds relationships with the young men and uses the opportunity to share the Gospel with them.

Outreach Idea #38: Spring Break Mission Trip. My parents were missionaries in Juarez, Mexico. For thirteen years our family hosted the sixth-grade class from Victory Christian Center in Tulsa, Oklahoma, and from Casey Treat's church in Seattle, Washington, for a Spring Break Mission Trip. The sixth graders started raising money for their mission trip at the beginning of the school year. Some years we had up to ninety sixth-graders and their parent sponsors come help us minister. We took them out into the poorest neighborhoods in Mexico and we went running through the streets inviting people to church. We visited schools, and orphanages, and we took the teams to minister in the Juarez dump where people dug through

trash with their hands in order to earn a living.

Outreach Idea #39: St. Patrick's Day - March 17. St. Patrick was an amazing man of God who preached to the pagan druids of Ireland and converted the whole island to Christianity. Use this holiday to tell his story and to reach out to the Irish community in your area.

April
Outreach Idea #40: Reach an Atheist Day - April 1. The first day of April is known as April Fool's Day. Psalm 14:1 says, "The fool has said in his heart there is no God." Use this day to target atheists with the Gospel. They will certainly not appreciate being called a "fool" so do not tell them why you are talking to them on this particular day.

Outreach Idea #41: Easter. After Christmas, Holy Week is the second most important time for evangelism. How do you celebrate Palm Sunday, Passover, Good Friday, and Easter Sunday? What can you do on these days to attract people to your church? What type of program can you offer that will get people to come back the week after Easter? Perhaps you could offer an Easter Sunrise Service or a drama about the passion of the Christ to attract people to come to your church.

Charles Neiman in El Paso, Texas often starts a catchy sermon series on Easter Sunday that continues for the next four weeks. If you can catch people's attention on Easter, they will continue to come back to your church in the weeks to come.

Outreach Idea #42: Easter Egg Hunt. Invite children to come to your church for an Easter Egg Hunt. Get families to come by offering significant prizes. Put cash or gift certificates in some of the candy eggs.

May

Outreach Idea #43: Cinco de Mayo - May 5. Use Cinco de Mayo to reach out to the Hispanic people in your neighborhood.

Outreach Idea #44: National Teacher Day. The first full week in May has been designated as National Teacher Appreciation Week in the United States. Do a special service to honor teachers. Ask every child in the church to invite his or her teacher to come to be honored.

Outreach Idea #45: National Day of Prayer - 1st Thursday in May. Use this day of prayer to pray for the lost to be saved.

Outreach Idea #46: Mother's Day – 2nd Sunday in May. Designate Mother's Day as a special day to lead mothers to Christ. Give prizes for the oldest mom, the mom with the most children, and the newest mother. Give a rose to every mother.

Outreach Idea #47: Armed Forces Day - 3rd Saturday in May. Honor all the troops who have served in the military.

Outreach Idea #48: Memorial Day - Last Monday in May. Honor the military on Memorial Day Weekend. Have a flag drill with local veterans. Sing the National Anthem.

June

Outreach Idea #49: Father's Day - 3rd Sunday in June. Designate Father's Day as a special day to honor fathers and lead them to Christ.

Outreach Idea #50: Vacation Bible School. This is a great way to reach out to your community. Get your whole church involved in inviting children to attend. If you win the kids, you will impact the whole family.

July

Outreach Idea #51: Independence Day - July 4 (Canada Day - July 1). Throw a patriotic party for your whole community. Wave lots of flags. Celebrate the history of your city.

Outreach Idea #52: Fireworks. Go to the fireworks display in your city and give away sparklers, or watermelon to all the people who have gathered together to watch the fireworks.

August

Outreach Idea #53: Back-to-School Celebration. Get school supply lists from local schools. Put together packets of pencils, pens, paper, bookmarks (with evangelistic info on them), rulers, scissors, and staplers. Go door-to-door and invite all the school-age children to your church for back-to-school Sunday.

September

Outreach Idea #54: Labor Day – 1st Monday in September. On Labor Day weekend, invite people from different professions to share about what they do. Set up booths honoring different professions like nursing, teaching, plumbing, electricians, etc. Invite people from each of these professions to come advertise at each booth. Invite construction workers to park their machinery in front of the church. Businesses love the opportunity to advertise and the church gets an opportunity to pull people into the church that normally never attend.

Outreach Idea #55: Grandparents' Day – Sunday following Labor Day. While we have a day to celebrate Mothers and Fathers, there's also one for celebrating grandparents. Use Grandparents Day to celebrate the people who brought our moms and dads into the world.

October
Outreach Idea #56: Trunk or Treat. Central Church in Tulsa, Oklahoma invites church members to decorate the trunks of their cars with games for children. Games include: Ring toss, Putt Putt Golf, Ball In Basket, Water Gun Shootout, and Fish 4 Candy. Dozens of children from the neighborhood come to play games and get free candy. They also have inflatable bounce toys, a petting zoo, and a hay ride. Inside the church is free chili and hotdogs.

Outreach Idea #57: Harvest Festival. Many churches throw a Halloween-alternative festival. Ask every family in the church to invite another family to attend. Here are some ideas for making it a successful outreach:
- Give away lots of candy.
- Set up games for children to play.
- Rent inflatables and carnival games.
- Have a petting zoo.
- Give prizes to children who dress like Bible characters or animals.

Outreach Idea #58: Halloween - October 31. One night a year, many people in your neighborhood are happy to open their doors to talk to you. Take their candy and give them a tract or a printed invitation to your church indicating location and service times. When children come to your door, give them candy and a church invitation.

November
Outreach Idea #59: Thanksgiving - 4th Thursday in November (in Canada: 2nd Monday in October). Give people in your community reasons to be thankful. Christ for the Nations Church in Dallas, Texas does a yearly Thanksgiving outreach. They set up a tent in an open field near a low-income apartment complex. They cook a complete Thanksgiving dinner and invite everyone to come. As

people are eating, they sing songs, do dramas, perform dances, entertain with jokes, and preach the Gospel.

Outreach Idea #60: Family Thanksgiving. On the Sunday before Thanksgiving, ask your church members to pray for their family members that are coming over for Thanksgiving dinner.

December
Outreach Idea #61: Christmas. December is the best month for evangelism. What is Christmas all about? This time of joyous celebration is a natural time of year to share the true Reason for the season. Friends, family, and co-workers may be more open to hearing the message of Christmas as hearts and minds turn toward the baby in the manger.

Outreach Idea #62: Christmas Cards. Print beautiful church Christmas cards. Include a brief Gospel message inside the card. Two weeks before Christmas, have a Christmas card party at your church. Everyone brings their address books and mails cards to all their friends and family. The church can provide the cards, writing materials, and have postage available for sale. Or send cards to everyone within a one-mile radius of your church. Ask church members to write a hand-written message inviting people to come visit the church on Christmas Eve.

Outreach Idea #63: Live Nativity Scene. A church in El Paso, Texas uses their entire congregation to stage a live nativity scene. Cars line up for blocks to get into their parking lot. Everyone drinks hot chocolate and walks through a tent where they experience the sights and sounds of first-century Bethlehem.

Outreach Idea #64: Christmas Caroling. Go door-to-door or visit a public area singing Christmas carols.

Outreach Idea #65: Christmas Around the World. Victory Christian Center in Tulsa, Oklahoma, hosts a yearly event where they invite different ethnic groups. People from dozens of different nations put together booths explaining the history, displaying artifacts, and serving food from their nation. As visitors stop at each booth, they get a stamp in a mini-passport. On the platform, performers showcase music and dances from different countries. This is a great way to pull in people from many different nations to your church.

Outreach Idea #66: Christmas Eve Candlelight Service. Many people only go to church once a year, and that once is on Christmas Eve. How can you make sure your Christmas Eve service is evangelistic in nature? Do not just light candles. Talk about Jesus, the Light of the world.

Outreach Idea #67: Christmas Day. Give Christmas gifts away in the neighborhood. Perhaps a DVD or CD of the church choir singing Christmas Carols. Every year, Victory Christian Center in Edmonton, Alberta, rents the convention center and feeds five thousand people on Christmas Day. Hundreds of volunteers work to serve the food.

Outreach Idea #68: New Year's Eve Countdown Party – December 31. Throw a big party on New Year's Eve. As you wait for the New Year to arrive, give people an opportunity to start a new life.

Outreach Idea #69: Focus on Outreach for an Entire Year. Jerry Beebe of Wenatchee First Assembly in Wenatchee, Washington, decided his church would do 12 outreaches in 2012. Each month he gave his church members an opportunity to participate in an outreach to the community. Each outreach usually had 15-20 participants. Different leaders got excited about different outreaches. He said at least one family joined his church because of each outreach.

Here are the outreaches that they did:

In January, the church did snow shoveling in the neighborhoods around the church. Here is how their church website described the outreach, "In January we will be going door-to-door throughout our community and shoveling snow for our neighbors. We aren't asking for money; we just want to be a blessing to them! We will be meeting on January 28th at 7:30 am at the church for a time of prayer and hot chocolate. From there we head out on our mission to bring a little relief to the people of our area!"

In February, the church offered free baby-sitting for couples who want to go on a Valentine's Day date.

In March, the fathers and sons in the church hosted a Pinewood Derby for the community. This is an event where a father and son make a racecar out of a block of wood and race it against other cars. The church website said, "It is a free event for our community and their goal was to get dozens of kids involved. The purpose behind Pinewood Derby is to help parents connect with their children. It gives a project for them to complete together, and a sense of accomplishment seeing that finished product fly down the track."

In April, the church did One Day to Feed the World. Pastor Jerry asked each member of the church to donate one day of wages to feed hungry people through Convoy of Hope. On this Sunday, the church collected the second biggest offering in its history. The people gave enough money to fill 57 pallets full of food, the equivalent of three semi-truck loads.

In May, the church decided to pick up trash. Every year, tens of thousands of people descend on the Wenatchee Valley to witness the Apple Blossom Grand Parade. The church was the last entry in the

parade, walking the streets with garbage bags and matching T-shirts with the church logo, smiling and collecting trash.

In June, the church had a "Summer Kick-off" Block Party.

In July, during the heat of the summer, the church reached out with a 4th of July Water Bottle Hand Out.

In August, the church hosted a Mega-Sports Camp. This was a modified Vacation Bible School where they offered training to kids in lacrosse, soccer, and basketball. At a sports camp you can provide a safe environment, promote team building, and show the love of Christ.

In September, the church Adopted a School. They went to the principal of a local elementary school and asked what they could do to serve. The principal replied, "We need some help with our landscaping." So the church planted flowers, pulled weeds, picked up trash, and put down mulch around all the trees at the school. In preparing for the outreach, a simple announcement was made in church that they needed, "Gloves, Rakes, Wheel Barrows, and a Good Attitude!"

In October, the church threw a Fall Harvest Party.

In November and December, the church had a "Be the Light" Holiday Catalog. Different needs in the community were featured in the bulletin and church members chose which need they wanted to fill. The featured needs ranged from taking a bag of groceries to a needy family, to buying a Christmas gift for a child, to giving the elderly a ride to their dentist or doctor appointments.

Section 4:
Sharing Your Faith

Outreach Idea #70: Operation Andrew. Billy Graham has frequently used Operation Andrew as a way to encourage believers to bring their friends, family, and neighbors to Christ. The name comes from Andrew, the disciple of Jesus, whom the Bible records brought his brother Peter to Jesus: *"One of the two who heard John speak, and followed Him, was Andrew, Simon Peter's brother. He first found his own brother Simon, and said to him, "We have found the Messiah" (which is translated, the Christ). And he brought him to Jesus"* (John 1:40-43 NKJV). We all know people who need Jesus. By using Operation Andrew we can pray for, invite, and bring people with us to church, outreach events, or small groups where they have an opportunity to hear the Gospel and get saved.

1. Look Around - Your mission field is right where you live, work, or go to school! List the names of individuals you know who need Jesus.

Write down the names of seven people who need Jesus, your "Seven for Heaven" list:
1.
2.
3.

4.
5.
6.
7.

2. Look Up - God changes people through prayer. Pray each day for each person on your list. Ask God to give you opportunities to share His love.

3. Look Out – Look for ways to cultivate friendships and earn confidence and trust. Invite people over for dinner or to a sporting event. Look for an opening to talk about Christ.

4. Look Forward - Begin to talk with each person on your list about visiting church with you. Choose a specific date, pray, and invite them. Offer to give them a ride.

5. Look After – Be prepared to encourage those who respond to Christ or show any interest in the Gospel. Continue to love and pray for those who do not respond. Remember to encourage each person on your list to attend your home church regularly.

Outreach Idea #71: Witnessing Door-to-Door. Despite the negative name Jehovah Witnesses and Mormons have given to witnessing door-to-door, knocking on doors is still an effective way to reach out to our communities.
Witnessing Tips:
* Survey your area. Find a large map of your city and highlight the areas you want to reach. Or you can use Google street view to determine the neighborhoods you want to visit. Start in areas near your church and work out from there. Set a goal of knocking on every door within a 5-mile radius of your church at least once each year.
* Have a planned time to go soul winning.

* Be clean and neat. Take breath mints along.
* Show yourself friendly. Be complimentary and gracious. Be bold, loving, humble, and enthusiastic. Stay calm, cool, and collected. Do not act crazy, mad, or frustrated.
* Be led by the Holy Spirit.
* Teams should go out two-by-two, the same way Jesus sent out the disciples. When you witness, one person should do the talking, the other should be praying inaudibly.
* Each group of two should be assigned to a larger team of 2-4 groups under the direction of an Evangelism Leader. These teams should begin and finish blocks together. One team should work on side of the street and the other team should work the other side. When in an apartment complex, the entire team should start together, work together, and finish together. Keep an eye on your team. Do not leave team members unaccounted for.
* Stay away from religious language and terminology. Focus on Jesus.
* Do not enter homes. Your job of witnessing and praying with people can be done from the doorstep.
* Introduce yourself and mention the name of your church. It is vital for people to understand who you are.
* If no one is home, leave a flyer about your church or a gospel tract in the door.
* Remember your purpose is to spread a message of God's love. Be respectful of the faith tradition of each person. If someone says they do not want you to pray for them, thank them for listening and move on to the next house. Your goal is to bring love, reconciliation, and hope to a neighborhood.
* You are like a farmer; you are sowing seeds of God's love. Some of those seeds will produce an immediate harvest; others will take longer to spring up.
* Be aware of your surroundings at all times. If you encounter resistance, it is best to leave. Do not get into arguments or engage in

conflict. If you encounter someone who has a mental disease, or is under the influence of drugs or alcohol, be careful.

* Follow up on each contact and invite them to come to church with you sometime in the next week. Pick them up for church if possible.

* Use a script for witnessing. Here is an example of what I have used. Feel free to develop your own.

Sample Script for Door-to-Door Witnessing

Hello, my name is [your name] and this is my friend [partner's name]. We are from [name of your church]. This neighborhood is on our heart and we want to pray for every person and family in this area.

Has anyone ever told you that God loves you and has a wonderful plan for your life? Can we ask you a quick but important question? If you were to die tonight, do you know for sure that you would go to heaven? (If they reply "yes" ask "Why do you say yes?" If they respond with anything but "I have Jesus in my heart" or something similar to that, proceed with the script. If they say "no" or "I hope so" proceed with the script.)

Let me quickly share with you what the Bible says. It reads, "All have sinned and come short of the glory of God" And "the wages of sin is death, but the gift of God is eternal life in Christ Jesus our Lord" It also reads, "Everyone who calls on the name of the Lord shall be saved."

Would you like to call on Jesus right now and make sure that you are saved by saying a short prayer with me? Say this with your heart and with your mouth so you can hear it.

"Dear God in Heaven, I call on Jesus right now to save me. I believe Jesus died on the cross to pay for my sin. I repent of all my sins. I

believe Jesus rose from the dead. Right now, I make Jesus the Lord of my life. I want to obey His word. Thank You God for setting me free. In Jesus' name I pray, Amen."

Is there anything specific that we can pray with you for? (Pray with them. Invite them to your church and get follow-up information: name, address, and phone number.)
Watch On-Line: http://www.youtube.com/watch?v=-U-dtd4L-vw

Outreach Idea #72: Friendship Evangelism. Evangelist Per Hyldgaard from Denmark explains that one of the best ways to reach people in Europe is through friendship evangelism. What does friendship evangelism look like?

1. First, start a hobby that can be helpful to building relationships with people. Watch birds, play a sport, start a knitting club, go ice fishing, etc. Use your hobby to meet new people and to build loving and caring relationships.

2. After you develop a friendship, look for an opportunity to share the Gospel. First, you earn the right to be heard, then you tell them about Jesus. As one pastor said, "If you want to bring someone with you to church, you have to earn the right to invite."

This method of outreach teaches church members to be evangelists all the time. Every Christian can be evangelistic in their lifestyle. Sometimes when we hold an evangelism service once a year, people focus on evangelism on that occasion and then feel like they do not need to do anything evangelistic the rest of the year.

By talking about friendship evangelism, we teach people to be salt and light at their workplace, at school, and in the community. Most Christian have too few friends out in the world. Christians need to

have a godly lifestyle but also be normal. Watch a movie every now and then. Go to a concert. Have a hobby. Enjoy life. Even though we are not of the world, we do live in the world, and we are here to reach the people of the world.

Live a lifestyle that smells good to people, then they will really like you. When a Christian exhibits good fruit, people will come and ask "Why are you so happy?" This question is a great opening for sharing the Gospel.

The church's job is to have relevant church services with relevant preaching so the church members can bring their friends.

Unfortunately, some people who focus on "friendship evangelism" never get to the evangelism part. If you are more worried about jeopardizing the friendship than you are about your friend going to hell, then you are not a true friend. Never let the friendship become more important than your friend's soul.

Three Scriptures to remember when telling your friends about your faith:
1. Never hide the Gospel from people. Jesus said, *"Nor do they light a lamp and put it under a basket, but on a lampstand, and it gives light to all who are in the house"* (Matthew 5:15).
2. Our goal is not to please men, but to please God. Paul said, *"For do I now persuade men, or God? Or do I seek to please men? For if I still pleased men, I would not be a bondservant of Christ"* (Galatians 1:10).
2. According to Ephesians 4:15, we are to speak the truth in love but we should never forget to speak the truth.

Outreach Idea #73: It's Real! Testimony Night. Per Hyldgaard from Denmark hosted a testimony night at his church. He invited a

policeman, a former criminal, a teacher, and a young person to share their personal stories of coming to faith in Christ. His church members invited their friends and neighbors to come hear the testimonies and to ask questions about God.

Outreach Idea #74: Power Evangelism. When Jesus sent the disciples out to preach the Gospel, he told them to *"heal the sick, cleanse the lepers, raise the dead, and cast out demons"* (Matthew 10:8). When you witness, instead of just speaking about God, why not demonstrate God? Pray for sick people and expect God to do a miracle. We have seen God do thousands of miracles in our Gospel Festivals: the blind see, the deaf hear, the cripples start to walk. Marilyn Hickey once said to me, "Miracles are the dinner bell that draw people to the banqueting table of heaven."

Outreach Idea #75: Servant Evangelism. Jesus said, *"The greatest in the kingdom is the servant of all"* (Matthew 23:11). Did you know that the word "servant" is mentioned 896 times in the New King James Version of the Bible? Find someone who has a need and help out. Mow a lawn. Clean a kitchen. Paint a house. Carry someone's groceries. Shovel a driveway. Find a way to serve. As you demonstrate the heart of a servant it will open the door for you to share the Gospel.

Outreach Idea #76: Share Your Testimony. Telling people your testimony is simple. It goes like this: who I was before I got saved + what Jesus did for me = my life now.

Outreach Idea #77: Use Your Job as a Platform. Roberta Potts is the daughter of famous evangelist Oral Roberts. She is a lawyer who specializes in representing people who have been in accidents. Almost everyone who comes into her office is suffering from pain. This gives Roberta the opportunity to share about God's ability to

heal people. Her father brought God's healing power to his generation and Roberta continues that tradition from the comfort of her office.

Outreach Idea #78: Community Survey. Evangelist Michael Lusk teaches churches how to do community surveys. Church members walk around a shopping center, park, or neighborhood with a clipboard full of questionnaires. They ask people about their spiritual state and at the end of the survey offer to pray with people for salvation. Here are some questions that work particularly well at Christmas time:

1.   Do you celebrate Christmas?
2.   What does Christmas mean to you?
3.   What was the purpose for Christ's birth?
4.   Have you come to a point in your spiritual life that if you died tonight, you would go to heaven?

Outreach Idea #79: Tracts. My grandfather was saved after he found a Gospel tract lying on the ground. He read it and decided to become a follower of Jesus. Because of his testimony, I believe strongly in the power of giving people the Gospel in written form. More than 100,000 of my tracts have now been printed.

Angelo Mitropoulos, in his book "The Power of Literature Evangelism," calls tracts "little preachers." He points out that Paul's written letters impacted far more people than his spoken sermons. If you have not been witnessing because you do not know how to approach strangers, a tract can be the "bait" that allows you to go fishing. Keep a stack of tracts handy in your pocket or purse to give to your friends, co-workers, waitresses, store clerks, and anyone else you run into.

A piece of paper can go farther than you can go, stay longer than

you can stay, and reach more people than you can reach. God sent His Son for a season, but He left His written Word for all of eternity.

T. L. Osborn writes in his book, "Soul Winning Out Where the Sinners Are," "The written Word knows no fear and flinches in the face of no man. It preaches the same message to the rich and to poor, to the king and to the commoner. It never loses its temper and never retaliates in anger. It takes no note of scoffs, jeers, or insults. It never tires, but works 24 hours a day, even while we sleep. It is never discouraged, but will tell its story over and over again. It will speak to one as willingly as to a multitude, to a multitude as readily as to one. It always catches a person in just the right mood to be receptive, for it only speaks as he chooses to listen. It can be received, read, and studied in secret. It gets undivided attention in the quiet hours. It speaks without a foreign accent. The written Word is more permanent than the human voice. It never compromises and never changes its message. It continues to speak and make its message plain, long after audible words have been forgotten and their sound has faded."

One enthusiastic believer went into public restrooms and unrolled several feet of toilet paper. Then, as he rolled the paper back up he inserted a Gospel tract every couple of feet. This is a great practical outreach because everyone who sits on the toilet wishes they had something to read.

Outreach Idea #80: Baptism Service. Luke Inberg, from The Father's House in Morinville, Alberta, recommends using a water baptism service as an opportunity to invite people who do not normally come to church. Each candidate for baptism is given invitation cards to give to friends and family to invite them to attend the ceremony. The baptism becomes a celebration. Before you baptize the candidates, ask them questions:
* How did you get saved?

* What does Jesus mean to you?
* What is your favorite scripture?
* What is God doing in your life?
* Why are you getting baptized today?

Outreach Idea #81: Baby Dedications. Another great occasion to invite people to church is when a family dedicates a baby. Encourage families to invite grandma and grandpa, aunts and uncles, cousins, etc. Before the service, have a special reception for the entire family. Use the occasion to explain the spiritual significance of dedicating a baby. This is a non-intrusive opportunity to invite extended family members to come to church.

Outreach Idea #82: "Cell"-vation Service. During our 2nd Annual Soul Winning Conference at Dr. Phillip Goudeaux's church in Sacramento, California, God gave us a tremendous idea for leading people to Jesus. We were taking people from the church out into the neighborhood, knocking on doors and witnessing. One pastor knocked on a door and the man who answered explained that he was already a Christian. But his son was not saved. So the pastor asked, "Can I talk to your son?" The man replied, "He's not here. He's in San Francisco." The pastor said, "Let's call him on your cell phone and talk to him about God right now." A few minutes later, over the cell phone, this pastor led the son to Jesus.

As we rejoiced over this testimony, we had the idea of using our cell phones in the middle of a church service to lead people to Jesus. That night, we invited everyone in the audience to pull out their cell phones. They lifted their cell phones in the air and we dedicated their cell phones as "gospel tools." We asked the Holy Spirit to give each person the name of someone to call who was ready to receive Jesus.

In order to remove the fear of not knowing what to say, we wrote a sample script and put it on the screens so everyone could see it. This is what the script said:

"Hello, This is [your name] and you've been on my heart lately. I want to let you know that I'm praying for you and I want to make real sure that you're going to heaven with me. Would you pray this prayer with me? Dear God in heaven I make Jesus the Lord of my life. I believe Jesus died on the cross to pay the price for my sins. I believe Jesus rose from the dead and right now I give my life to Jesus Christ. Amen."

People flipped open their phones and began calling their friends and family. As soon as someone answered, they began reading the script. If no one answered, they left a message or texted them the script instead. Several people called back later to report they prayed the prayer.

We invited every person who led someone to the Lord on his or her cell phone to stand up and to come to the platform. After about three or four minutes people began popping up and running to the platform, many of them were very emotional. They were crying, they were laughing, some of them were dancing, and we began to hear testimonies.

One woman ran up shouting, "I have prayed for my mother for 20 years; she just gave her life to Jesus!" Another man called his brother who was in the middle of a fistfight with his wife; the brother gave his life to Jesus Christ. One thirteen-year-old boy called five of his school friends and led all five of his friends to Jesus. The man sitting next to us led two of his employees to Jesus. Aunts and uncles, brothers and sisters, fathers and mothers, grandmas and grandpas, friends, and co-workers were saved. It was a divine move of the

Holy Spirit. At the first "cell"-vation service in history, the Tuesday night of the "Soul Winning Conference," 195 people gave their lives to Jesus. A few days later, we held another "cell"-vation service at Dr. Goudeaux's south campus, and 232 people gave their lives to Jesus. And again the next Sunday in an evening service at a small church in central California, 14 people gave their lives to Jesus from an audience of about 20 people using the "cell"-vation call. And since that day, over and over again we've seen this evangelism idea work.

This is a tremendous way for churches to empower their congregation members to be soul winners. The problem with soul winning is that most Christians don't actively lead others to Jesus. They know they should look for opportunities to witness, but it's very difficult for them to find those opportunities or to really feel comfortable leading people to Jesus. In a corporate atmosphere it is much easier to step out of a comfort zone and witness. God gives a corporate anointing in the service for leading the lost to Christ.

Everyone has at least one or two people in their phone list who do not know Jesus. It is worth giving them a call. Many of the believers at our service led family members to Jesus. They had been praying for their family members for 20 years, but had never witnessed to them. In one night we turned an entire church into a church of soul winners. Many of the people who were present that night had never prayed a prayer of salvation with anyone before, and for the first time they had the joy of introducing someone to God. This is an idea that can be done in every single church, at least once a year. Churches should regularly have a "cell"vation service. The whole church can bring their Rolodex, their business contacts, their phones, and call someone who needs salvation. End the "cell"-vation service with a "cell"-ebration, letting people share testimonies of those who received salvation! This outreach is off the hook.

Section 5:
Meet a Need

Outreach Idea #83: Car Wash. In conjunction with The Father's House Christian Fellowship, I took a team of teenagers to La Loche, Saskatchewan, to minister to a First Nation's people group. One effective outreach we did was a car wash. We stationed teenagers on the corner in front of the church with signs advertising a free car wash. As cars pulled up, we not only soaped, rinsed, and polished their vehicle, but we also offered them free hot dogs as they waited. And on top of all that, the waiting period provided a great opportunity for team members to offer to pray with the people who had come to get a car washed. In a community that has a deep distrust of outsiders, this outreach allowed us to show the love of Christ in a practical way. Watch On-Line: http://www.youtube.com/watch?v=gQHFu0ErYPc

Outreach Idea #84: Clothing Drive. Ask everyone in the church to empty their closets of quality items they no longer wear and to donate their clothes to the church. Do an outreach to a less fortunate neighborhood or the homeless and give away the clothing.

Outreach Idea #85: Yard Sale. Daci-vawn Deveaux's church collected nice clothes, shoes, baby items, toys, cookware, furniture, computers, cribs, and toiletries. They cleaned and ironed each piece

of clothing and polished all the furniture. They advertised the yard sale throughout their neighborhood, and, on the day of the event, church parishioners were on hand to assist the shoppers. They sold everything inexpensively and used the opportunity to talk to people from the community one-on-one.

Outreach Idea #86: Food Ministry. Barry Habib in New Jersey houses a food ministry in his church. Most of the food is donated by various grocery stores and government entities. Because he accepts government assistance with the food bank, he is not allowed to require people to listen to a religious message in order to receive the food but he is allowed to offer to pray for people. Every Wednesday morning, over one hundred people visit his church in order to receive food.

The Great Commission is to "Go into all the world and preach the Gospel." The Great Commandment is to "Love your neighbor as you love yourself." Both are equally important. However, when you feed people, do not forget to introduce them to Jesus. If you feed and clothe a man but fail to share the Gospel with him, ultimately all you have done is made him warmer and well fed on his journey to hell.

Outreach Idea #87: Nursing Home Outreach. Rodney Howard-Browne gives the following tips for visiting nursing homes:

* When you call the nursing home, ask to speak to the activities director: "Hello, my name is [your name] and I am calling from [your church name]. I am calling you today because God has put the elderly on my heart and I would like to have the opportunity to come into your facility and offer prayer to your residents. Our teams are well training in terms of HIPPA laws (not taking names or private information). They are polite and not pushy. They wear name tags, knock on doors to the resident's rooms, and will check in at each

nursing station."

* Most facilities are thankful that you desire to come into their nursing home and pray with their patients.

* They can either gather together a group of senior citizens, or your team can go door-to-door praying for the patients. Many of the people who most need prayer are not able to participate in group settings due to their physical ailments.

* Make sure to ask what time(s) work best for your teams to visit. The times that work well for many facilities are 10 am, 1 pm, 2:30 pm, and 4 pm.

* It is important to stop at each individual nursing station and let them know you are offering prayer for the patients.

* Knock loudly at each door because many of the patients have trouble hearing.

* Pray for the sick and expect God to do miracles.

* Many of the patients may be sleeping. Often this is not because they are sick, it is because they are bored. They have nothing to do all day so they sleep. Gently wake them up so you can talk to them about Jesus.

* To follow-up, keep going back to the nursing home on a regular basis to do a service for the residents.

Andrew Walker worked in nursing homes for fifteen years. He gives the following helpful tips for doing nursing home ministry:

1. Many if not all nursing homes are grateful that you want to come in and have an activity with their residents. Many homes will ask you to schedule a couple times a month and some even desire a once-a-week outreach, depending on how many other churches come in to their home.

2. When doing a time of praise and worship or Bible study, be sure to schedule a room in the facility for you to have your group meeting in. Make sure you put in the schedule that you will be visiting room-

to-room and the approximate timeframe you will be visiting rooms. It's important that you stick to the schedule you gave the home as they might have other activities that day on the schedule.

3. Try to schedule the time that you are there in the mid-morning or mid-afternoon, when you go there after supper a lot of the residents retire to their rooms for the rest of the evening and don't like to get out.

4. When praying for residents be sure to check with the nurse's desk on that wing to make sure there isn't a room they do not want you to enter, due to sickness or other reasons.

5. Be sure to wear your name tags as the residents always want to know who you are and where you are from.

6. Be sure to knock on their doors loudly and to speak loudly, slowly and clearly as many residents are challenged with hearing.

7. If the resident is resting and does not want to be bothered, please do not persist, just quietly leave and respect their privacy.

8. Always be respectful using "yes ma'am" or "yes sir." Elderly folk love polite people and they will be more open to talk to you if you are polite.

9. When praying for a resident always make it short and to the point. Expect God to work a miracle in their life no matter how aged they are.

10. When leading a resident to the Lord, have a salvation book to give them and show them that reading the little book will get them started on their journey with the Lord.

11. After praying with them always ask if you can make a follow-up visit with them in a week or so. If they say "yes," be sure to follow-up as they will be counting on you to come back.

12. Before leaving, put chairs and tables back in the spot they were in if you moved them. Make sure you leave the area you used in clean and orderly manner.

13. As you leave, thank the activities director or whoever you had contact with for allowing you to be there for a couple of hours.

14. If you make a schedule to come back, be sure to always keep that schedule and be there when you say you will be there. The activities director usually tells the residents a day or so in advance that you are coming, so the residents will be looking forward to your visit.

Outreach Idea #88: Rehabilitation House. Provide a place for drug addicts, alcoholics, ex-prisoners, and vagrants to get clean. Each day the recovering addicts spend time in the Word of God, prayer, and worship. They could care for animals, tend gardens, or help maintain buildings. Give them accountability and close supervision.

Outreach Idea #89: Dream Center. Tommy Barnett started the Los Angeles Dream Center and it is now pastored by his son, Matthew Barnett. Now many churches across America have started Dream Centers of their own. The Tulsa Dream Center is in north Tulsa, an area with high crime and low incomes. They offer adult computer classes, athletics, after-school programs, drug rehabilitation, a medical clinic, a clothing ministry, a food ministry, and legal advice. Visit their website at www.tulsadreamcenter.org.

Outreach Idea #90: Give an Abused Person a Home to Live In. Pastor Greg Ables was riding around with a cop when the officer received a call from a "boobie bar." When they got there, a seventeen-year-old girl had lied about her age in order to become an exotic dancer. Her boyfriend had talked her into doing the job in order to make some money. He did not think she was dancing seductively enough so he beat her and gave her a black eye. Pastor Greg got on the phone and called an eighty-year-old women in his congregation. He said, "Betty, sorry to wake you up at two a.m. in the morning. I am at a boobie bar right now." She said, "Pastor, what are you doing at a boobie bar?" He said, "There is a seventeen-year-old girl here that needs some love. Can you come help me?" Thirty minutes later,

a Buick Century pulled up to the bar, and out stepped Grandma Betty resplendent in fuzzy slippers and hair rollers, and asked, "Where is that baby girl?" She put her arm around the teenager and helped her get into her car. Grandma Betty "adopted" the girl and let her stay in her home for over a year. After that she helped finance the girl's college education.

Outreach Idea #91: Prayer Call Center. Advertise a phone number people can call who need prayer. Man the phone lines with volunteers from the church. This is a great ministry opportunity for the elderly or shut-ins to minister to people.

Outreach Idea #92: Adopt-A-Block. Healing Place Church in Baton Rouge, Louisiana started a "Servolution," a church revolution through serving people. Find a poor neighborhood and "Adopt-a-Block." Take rakes, shovels, and trash bags. Pick up trash, paint people's houses, mow lawns, plant flowers, or offer to clean up people's kitchens. People do not care how much you know until they know how much you care. When you help people in your community, hearts will become receptive to your message. Could you and your congregation "Rock-a-Block" for Jesus?

At the Tulsa Dream Center Adopt-a-Block program they say, "The beauty of Adopt-a-Block is that a person does not have to be a highly-trained minister in order to take part. Anyone who loves God, loves people, and has a willingness to serve can play a vital role in this ministry. Contributions start as small as a smile and include things from making conversation or playing with children to helping out around the yard and house. If people in your congregation can bake cookies, play basketball, or just make someone feel special, they are more than qualified to be used in this ministry. Every Christian is qualified to show love to the hurting. The blocks are the perfect arena to discover and use the individual talents God has

designed in each person."

Outreach Idea #93: Pick Up Trash. Give everyone in the church a plastic bag and send them to the park to pick up trash. Use the opportunity to strike up conversations with people.

Outreach Idea #94: Light up the World. Kevin Wagner suggests going to the store and buying $20 worth of light bulbs. Late on Saturday morning, pick a neighborhood, split up into teams of two, and go door-to-door asking people if they need any light bulbs in the house replaced. Assure them that your offer is completely free. After you have finished replacing a burned-out bulb with a new one, tell the family about Jesus, the "Light of the world."

Outreach Idea #95: Pet Adoption Day. Debbie Webb suggests teaming up with a local animal shelter to find homes for our four-legged friends. The church could offer to set up a tent in their parking lot and use it to showcase the homeless animals. As people arrive to look at the animals, volunteers could share each animal's story and also share the Gospel. The event could be advertised by posting flyers in veterinary offices and pet groomer's salons.

Outreach Idea #96: Seminars. Host a seminar where you give people valuable information to help them in areas where they have a specific need. People who do not come to church on Sunday morning may be willing to come in order to learn about a specific topic. Here are some seminar topics you could offer:
* Marriage Seminar
* Business Seminar
* Health and Nutrition Seminar
* Parenting Seminar
* Coping with Depression Seminar
* Overcoming Grief Seminar

* Freedom from Addiction Seminar
* Learn a Foreign Language Seminar
* Learn English as a Second Language Seminar

Outreach Idea #97: Host a Financial Skills Seminar. This is not a teaching series on tithing. Teach people how to write a budget, build a savings account, write a will, and invest their money. Dave Ramsey's Financial Peace University is a great program that helps people get out of debt and build wealth and financial security.

Section 6:
Be Social

Outreach Idea #98: Appreciation Meals for Law Enforcement Personnel. Pastor Greg Ables from Newspring Family Church in Jenks, Oklahoma, started doing a luncheon for local cops once a month at his church. The policemen said, "Pastor, we don't want to be preached at." Greg promised to never preach at them and he even promised to never even pray over the meal. Some of the members of his congregation got upset and said, "We have to pray for the food. What if one of them gets sick?" But Greg stuck with his promise to the cops. At the first lunch, only twenty cops showed up but as word spread, over one hundred and twenty cops attended. Frequently cops ask Greg (who they affectionately call "Preacher") to ride with them in their cars. Usually, it is because the cop wants to talk about something that is going on in their life. Over a four-year period, sitting in the front seat of patrol cars, Greg led 63 policemen to Jesus.

Every Thanksgiving, Abundant Living Faith Center in El Paso, Texas, takes a meal of turkey, dressing, cranberry sauce, and all the fixings to the local police stations and fire stations near their church. This has given them a lot of favor with law enforcement in El Paso.

Outreach Idea #99: Take Business Men and Women out for Lunch. Do you want lawyers, doctors, and CEO's to attend your

church? What are you doing to reach out to professional people?

1. Drive to the area where your business people work.
2. Ask your businessmen to invite some friends to the lunch.
3. Pay for lunch. Remember, this is your opportunity to reach out. If you invite someone to lunch, it is rude to let the bill sit there until the person you invited finally picks it up. Be quick to write the check and your businessmen will appreciate your generosity. The seed of a single lunch could result in a businessman tithing to your church for many years.
4. During the meal, do not talk about all your church projects and needs. Instead, build a relationship. Ask questions. Offer to pray for his family and his business.

Outreach Idea #100: Host a Block Party. I was invited to participate in a local church outreach in Glenpool, Oklahoma, with First Grace Church. The church has over one hundred members. Glenpool is a city of 12,000 people so the church feels it does not have the resources to do an outreach to the entire city, but they chose a particular neighborhood of about 150 homes to focus on.

The church rented inflatables and a popcorn machine, gave out hotdogs that had been donated for the event, invited a clown to make balloons, and had face painting available. They also did a raffle for a $300 pre-paid VISA card in order to attract adults. In advance of the block party, church members spread out into the community and invited people to come for free event. Of the 70 people who came around 25 people got saved! On Sunday morning, 8 people from the community came to church. At least two new families started attending the church. For a church of this size, this was a very successful evangelistic outreach.

Every church should give their congregation opportunities to reach out to those who are lost. Not every member of your church is called

to be an evangelist, but every member of your church can be involved in evangelism. By scheduling regular outreaches your church members can have an outlet for their ministry gifts. Whether they participate by cooking hotdogs, knocking on doors, playing music, or just hugging people, every person in the church, from the young to the old, can help win the lost to Christ.

Watch On-Line:
http://www.youtube.com watch?v=RMaFY4BlNOE

Outreach Idea #101: Cooking Classes. Paul Harbaugh points out that many serious health issues today—such as obesity and diabetes—can be traced to improper eating habits. Your church could offer cooking classes to help people learn how to cook healthy and nutritious meals. Teach basic nutrition, proper seasoning techniques, and basic cooking methods such as sauté, roast, braise, broil, boil, simmer, bake, etc. Ask local grocery stores to donate food.

Outreach Idea #102: Circus Family Night. My brother Stephen and I started "Clowns 4 Christ" when we were teenagers. We put on face paint, dressed up as clowns, and used juggling, unicycles, puppets, and magic tricks to entertain and minister to families. One summer, when I was sixteen and Stephen was twelve, we drove from El Paso, Texas, to Washington D.C., ministering along the way in churches across America. The Circus Family Night was billed as "exciting fun-filled entertainment" for the whole family. Each church printed circus tickets and handed them out in the community. The church was decorated as a circus tent and popcorn and cotton candy were served. We sang songs, played games, and preached the Gospel. Thousands of children gave their lives to Jesus because of these outreaches.

Outreach Idea #103: Visiting Homes. I recently attended a church growth conference in North America where complex strategies for

church planting were discussed. I heard workshops on effectively using the Internet, media, and newspaper advertising to attract people to church. But, no one mentioned the strategy used by my friend from India. His church growth method involves the habit of jumping on a motorbike and visiting homes from early in the morning until late in the evening every day of the week.

Surendra Kumar is building the Kingdom of God with painstaking patience. He pastors a church of forty people in Vijayawada, India, and leads several additional congregations that meet in people's homes. Pastor Kumar has no car; he uses a motorbike to travel to a different village every week for an evangelistic outreach. He only has two rooms in his rented home, but he has dedicated one of those rooms as a prayer room so that Hindus from his neighborhood can come for prayer.

There is often a great price to be paid for winning souls. In broken English, Pastor Kumar explained to me how he leads Hindu families to Jesus. First, he finds a Hindu family that is in need. He builds a relationship with the family by visiting their house on a weekly basis. Once he is a friend, he starts sharing the Gospel. He tells them stories about what Jesus did in the Bible. When a member of the family gets sick, he prays for a miracle. Pastor Kumar explains, "When the family sees the power of God, then they are willing to become followers of Jesus." In many cases, six to twelve months pass before the family asks to be baptized.

Pastor Kumar took me to visit one of the Hindu families that recently decided to follow Jesus. They showed me the alcove next to their front door where an idol once stood. Now a picture of Jesus has replaced the idol. The whole family decided to be baptized into the Christian faith. Now they are inviting neighbors over to their house to hear stories about Jesus.

I asked the father of the family about his journey to Jesus. He replied, "My brother's daughter was sick and in the hospital. She needed an operation that cost one lakh rupees (about $2,000). Pastor Kumar came and prayed for her in the name of Jesus and she was miraculously healed. When I saw the miracle, I wanted to know more about Jesus. I invited Pastor Kumar to visit my home, and when we heard about the power of Jesus, we decided to forsake our idols and become believers in Jesus."

Why is Pastor Kumar a success? First, he genuinely cares about people. Second, he builds relationships that become bridges to share the good news. Third, he relies on the power of God to convince people of the truth of God's Word. Fourth, he is willing to work in difficult conditions to lead people to Jesus. Perhaps we should use some of his methods to reach people right in our hometowns.

Watch On-Line: http://www.youtube.com/watch?v=I81_1oLo-Hs

Outreach Idea #104: Go Where the Sinners Are. James Buster of El Paso, Texas, owns a tattoo parlor. Frequently he has the opportunity to witness while he is inking a tattoo on one of his customers. Once a lesbian couple (one was an atheist, the other was Muslim) came to get matching tattoos. James told them how much God loves them and at first they refused to hear anything he had to say but he kept repeating, "God loves you, God loves you," and as the anointing of God filled the room, one of the girls started to cry. Both girls prayed with James to receive salvation.

James has a small group of believers who meet in his house once a week for a Bible study. He told them his witnessing stories and they got excited about telling people about Jesus. James started going to the hospital and praying for people. One time he prayed for a man who was sick with diabetes. The man's brother-in-law turned out to

be the coordinator of Texas Showdown Tattoo and Music Festival, a yearly event that draws over 15,000 people to El Paso.

The brother-in-law invited James to come pray for people at the Tattoo Festival. James was given two booths for free in the food vending area. At his booths, he raffled off a free tattoo. Over thirty volunteers from his church came and asked people if they wanted a free tattoo, then as people signed up, the volunteer asked if they needed prayer. In three days, James' team prayed with over 1,500 people for salvation. The coordinator of the tattoo festival said he had previously invited churches to come minister at his event but no churches took him up on his offer because they were scared of all the weird people with tattoos and body piercings. It took a person like James to go to the people who need God the most. Now, James offers a free tattoo of two nails in the shape of a cross to anyone who wants one.

Outreach Idea #105: Host a Sporting Event for International Students. Mangthang Haokip is an international student who loves soccer. He thinks churches should host a soccer tournament, a baseball game, a basketball 3-on-3 competition, or a cricket match in order to reach out to people from other nations. The church can provide water, referees, food, and a facility for the sporting event to take place. A prize can be given to the winning team. It can be advertised at local community colleges and the Gospel can be shared with the internationals who attend.

Outreach Idea #106 Family Movie Day. As an outreach to the community, Darren Warn suggests showing a movie at the church or renting out a local theater. Free hot dogs, popcorn, and drinks help attract people. Tickets are used as promotional tools. The movie can be a Christian movie or a movie with spiritual themes. Afterward, spend some time talking about the movie and use the lessons from

the movie to lead into a presentation of the Gospel.

Open Bible Faith Fellowship of Canada says, "We love a good movie, especially when it's a great message packaged in a story that is family-friendly. We've compiled a list of titles that you can choose from. Some are well-known like Facing the Giants and FireProof, but there are some lesser known titles that provide great entertainment along with a valuable lesson. Be sure to obtain a movie license before presenting to your congregations." Here are some of the movies that they suggest:

25 Hill
Christmas with a Capital "C"
Christmas Candle
Courageous
Facing the Giants
FireProof
Flywheel
God's Not Dead
Heaven is for Real
Last Ounce of Courage
Luther
No Greater Love
Prodigal
October Baby
Seven Days in Utopia
The Genesis Code
The Grace Card
To Save a Life
Unstoppable

Outreach Idea #107: Church Carnival. Hire rides, a petting zoo, and inflatable bounce toys and invite the community to come for

free. Give away food and prizes. During the middle of all the fun, do not forget to tell people how to get to heaven.

Outreach Idea #108: Car Show. South Tulsa Baptist Church in Tulsa, Oklahoma, hosts an annual Car Show. They offer prizes to various categories of classic automobiles. Several hundred car enthusiasts from the surrounding community come to show their cars and to see others. The event is staffed by volunteers from the church who look for opportunities to pray with people and to witness to them.

Outreach Idea #109: Rebuild a Car. For the past ten years, Jason Hunget has used his love of rebuilding cars to witness to people. He bought his first Camaro, a 1986 IROC-Z, in 1999. He used it to reach out to the drag racing community. Young men frequented his garage to hang out and help out with the car. This gives him time to lead them to Jesus and get them revved up about God.

Outreach Idea #110: Welcome Teams. Put together a team of volunteers who set aside one night each week to visit people who have visited the church in the past week(s).

Outreach Idea #111: Dance Night. Marla Creswell is from a rural town in western Oklahoma. In small towns like Marla's, towns of under 400, there is not much to do on a Friday night. Many people head to the bar to dance; others drink beer and drive the back-country roads. Her idea is to give people an alternative to going to the bar. Open up the church, rewrite the lyrics to worldly country songs, and invite people to a line dance. Not only does it give people an alternative to the bar atmosphere, but it gives your church an opportunity to get to know people in the community who otherwise might not go to a church.

Outreach Idea #112: All-Night Lock-In. Host an all-night party at your church for young people. Have a band, play games like basketball and dodgeball, provide lots of snacks and drinks, do dramas, show a movie. And preach the Gospel.

Outreach Idea #113: Ice Cream Social. Offer whipped cream, cherries, syrup, sprinkles, and different flavors of ice cream. Advertise "Free Sundaes on Sunday."

Outreach Idea #114: Fiesta. Pastor Isaias Sanchez at Lord of the Harvest Church in Corpus Christi, Texas says his people love to invite their friends to a big fiesta at the church. The church serves home-cooked Mexican food. While people eat, the youth put on a live drama performance of an evangelistic story like "The Cross and the Switchblade."

Section 7:
Go into the World

Outreach Idea #115: Church in the Park. By doing a church service in the local park you allow people to see what one of your church services is like without them facing the scary prospect of coming into an unfamiliar building. Have a potluck or picnic after the service and invite others in the park to join you.

Outreach Idea #116: Join a Local Event. The town of Atoka, Tennessee, has a yearly Halloween party. Pastors Jesse and Sharon Laney decided that instead of preaching against the evils of Halloween that they would use the holiday as an opportunity to share the Gospel. Every year they sponsor a booth at the event and church members give away candy, paint faces, and minister through puppets and drama. One participant said, "It is so neat to see a group of little goblins and witches pray with us for salvation."

Outreach Idea #117: Parade. Parades are a great time to reach out as families often come out to celebrate important events in their community. Why not be a part of it? 3 ways that your church could be part of a parade in your community are:
1.   Decorate a church float for a local parade.
2.   March in a parade with matching T-Shirts.
3.   Volunteer to clean up all the trash after a parade.

Outreach Idea #118: Water Give-Away. The entire church attends a local parade and gives away bottles of water to people who are thirsty. Order water bottles with a label advertising the church. As you give away drinking water, perhaps some people will discover the living water that only comes from Jesus.

Outreach Idea #119: Rent a Booth at Your Local Flea Market or State Fair. A ministry team sat at a booth all day long at the Tulsa State Fair and prayed for anyone who needed prayer. They also gave away free Bibles and literature to those who had questions. More than a million people visit the State Fair every year, so this outreach gave them an opportunity to minister to thousands of people over the course of the ten-day event.

Outreach Idea #120: Prophetic Evangelism. Ken Wood from Oklahoma City does a unique outreach at the Renaissance Fair. After noticing a fortuneteller who frequented the event, he asked organizers if his church could set up a tent. The sign out front announces, "Dreams, Prophecies, and Healing." As people enter the tent, church members greet each visitor and offer to interpret a dream. They listen to the dream and then ask the Holy Spirit for an insight into the meaning of the dream. Sometimes, God gives them a scripture for the person, other times God gives them a word of knowledge or a word of wisdom. After giving the interpretation, they ask the person if they want to give their life to Christ. In one day, Pastor Ken and his team of prophetic evangelists prayed with 405 different individuals.

A prophetic ministry team from Joseph's Storehouse in Edmonton, Alberta, operates a booth at various city festivals in the summer, advertising "Free Interpretation of Dreams." This attracts people who are "New Age" and open to the spiritual world. The ministers listen to the dream, pray for the interpretation, and give the meaning

by the Holy Spirit. Then they are able to pray for the seeker and present the Gospel.

Outreach Idea #121: Take a Short-Term Mission Trip. How will preaching in a foreign nation help your local church grow? The light that shines farthest shines brightest near at home. I have led hundreds of short-term trips over the past twenty years and the people who go on our trips always have life-changing experiences. They go home saying, "I am so thankful for how good we have it in North America" and they get fired up about reaching their own towns and cities for Jesus.

Outreach Idea #122: Bus Ministry. Rod Baker was the Education Director at Victory Christian Center in Tulsa, Oklahoma, for many years. He pioneered bus ministry, which is bussing low-income children to church in order to minister to them. Here are some ideas how you can start a bus ministry at your church:
1. Appoint a Bus Captain for each bus. His/her job is to greet people as they get on and to keep order as the driver drives.
2. Consistency is important.
3. Get a signed permission slip from parents before you give a ride to children.

Pastor Dan Olson from Living Word Church in Branson West, Missouri, has held a bus outreach to the children of his community every month for thirteen years. Many people in his area struggle with poverty and meth addiction. The church started with one small bus and now they run four buses and a van. Over forty volunteers from the church work to make the outreach happen. One Saturday morning each month, church members gather at seven in the morning. Some start cooking a meal to feed the children and others get on buses to go pick up the children. The children arrive by nine o'clock for a fun-filled, exciting time of ministry that includes balloons, puppets,

clowns, dramas, and a presentation of the Gospel. Afterwards, the church feeds all the kids, fills their pockets with candy, and drives them back home. Over the years, 926 children have given their lives to Jesus. One girl named Amber got saved at the age of nine after arriving at the church on a bus. Today, Amber is the church secretary and is married to a man who volunteers as the church's graphic artist. She loves helping with the bus ministry outreach, especially when little girls just like her get saved.

Outreach Idea #123: Tent Crusade. My father, Robert King, was inspired by videos of sinners walking "the sawdust trail" to get saved at Oral Roberts' tent crusades in the 1950's. He raised the money to purchase a tent that seats 300 people from the Miami Missionary Tent Company. He found a low-income housing project in Tulsa, Oklahoma, and set the tent up and began ministering to anyone who would come.

One day, my father invited Billy Joe Daugherty to come preach at the tent crusade. After Pastor Billy Joe saw the effectiveness of the tent ministry, he committed to doing one tent crusade each month in a different housing project in Tulsa. Victory Christian Center continued to hold tent crusades every month for over ten years.

My father took his big blue and white tent to Mexico and used it for evangelistic meetings in the barrios of Juarez, Chihuahua. Our family helped plant over forty churches using the tent as a Gospel net. It proved to be an effective tool for attracting people to hear the Good News.

Outreach Idea #124: March for Jesus. In 1994, the first global "March for Jesus" covered every time zone and involved over ten million Christians in over 170 different nations. Although the original organization that hosted "March for Jesus" disbanded after 2000,

churches can still march for Jesus through their local communities. Take your church members outside the walls of the church and do a parade through the center of your town. Lift up the name of Jesus through songs, banners, and signs.

Outreach Idea #125: Flash Mob. Mark Swiger did an evangelistic "flash mob" in Germany. He started an event on Facebook to recruit believers to come to a downtown plaza at a certain time. Over 300 Christians from various churches showed up dressed in red shirts (red to symbolize the blood of Jesus). At a given signal, they performed a coordinated song and dance (learned from a video posted on You-Tube). All the people in the plaza stopped to watch. Immediately after the song was finished, the believers sat down on the ground and Mark jumped up on the edge of a fountain and quickly presented the Gospel using a small sound system. He finished by saying, "If you need prayer, just ask anyone who is wearing a red shirt." Because of this impromptu evangelism, many people requested prayer in one of the most secular nations in the world. Watch online: http://www.youtube.com/watch?v=0ODvK25kJhw

Outreach Idea #126: Go Clubbing. Brian Stanart has a heart for taking teams to the Blue Dome District in downtown Tulsa, a lively nightlife area with lots of bars, coffeehouses, and clubs. He recommends going in groups of 3-4 and sitting down with people and witnessing to them. This type of outreach can lead to long philosophical discussions with people who are mostly drunk. Jesus was the "Friend of sinners"--shouldn't we be willing to go where the sinners are?

Outreach Idea #127: Silence Out Loud. According to Karen Castro, this outreach works well in a crowded area. A team of volunteers wears blue jeans and matching T-Shirts. The shirts have scenes of tsunamis, tornados, bombs, starvation, abortion, human trafficking,

etc. They each place a piece of bright red tape over their mouths. In bold letters, the tape reads "LIFE." The participants do not talk but they do have cards that explain the Gospel message. They walk around and show the cards to curious people. At a central location, a prayer booth can be erected so people can receive prayer.

Outreach Idea #128: Fight Night. Madison Welche suggests visiting a neighborhood and handing out flyers inviting people to a boxing match. Set up a boxing ring. Do a skit about a kid fighting the devil. When it looks like the kid is about to lose, God comes and picks up the kid and puts him on His shoulders. God knocks out the devil. Preach about how God helps us defeat the devil. Afterwards, let the kids come into the ring and play a boxing video game.

Outreach Idea #129: Witness Wear. Make church T-Shirts that will give people an opportunity to talk about God. Here are some ideas for one-liners to put on the front of your shirt:
• Ask me why I'm smiling.
• If you were killed and eaten by a zombie, would you go to heaven?
• Eternity is forever. Where will you spend it?
• "Is prayer your steering wheel or your spare tire?" (Corrie Ten Boom)
• Prayer works. I know.
• Jesus is a personal Friend of mine.
• Live for Jesus - Live Forever
• Miracles Happen
• One Way: JESUS (Graphic: Hand with index finger pointing heavenward)
* God Loves You and I'm Trying!
* Friends don't let friends go to hell.
* Don't put a question mark where God puts a period!

Outreach Idea #130: Art. St. Francis of Assisi said, "Always preach

the Gospel, and when necessary use words." Art is a great way to use our God-given creativity to impact a sight-and-sound generation. Scott Howe is using art to open conversations about God.

Scott was a passive atheist for many years. God supernaturally took him out of a dark world filled with sex and drugs in the music and club scene, and brought him into His marvelous light. Scott immediately started witnessing in bars and clubs and passing out tracks on the streets. God put it on his heart to do creative outreaches like art shows, poetry readings, and rap and rock concerts in order to reach a visual and experiential, post-modern culture.

After working for Reinhard Bonnke for several years, Scott launched his ministry, "Evoke," a creative evangelistic ministry. "Evoke" mobilize poets, dancers, artists, musicians, DJ's, visual artists, designers, camera operators, video editors, painters, photographers, illustrators, skateboarders, writers, filmmakers, visionaries, sculptors, anyone gifted with and exercising a creative or technical gift. They do art shows and street witnessing in Orlando, Florida. They hit beaches, boardwalks, art festivals, universities, and parties. As people look at their Gospel-centered art, it sparks interest in God and gives the artists an opening to share the salvation message.

Outreach Idea #131: Use Music. The worship leader at Jules Randrianjoary's church in Paris, France decided to ask local cafés if her worship team could play Christian music in front of the cafés. She asked permission from several café owners, but they all said "No." Finally, one café agreed. The café gave her permission to run an extension cord for electricity and her team set up their drums on the sidewalk. When they started to play, a crowd of French people quickly gathered and listened to the music. The team shared brief testimonies between the songs and they prayed for one Frenchman to receive salvation. The café owner liked the music so much that he

invited them to come back every Friday night to play inside the café.

Outreach Idea #132: The God Mobile In Seattle, Washington is a group that sets up a booth at fairgrounds. They have a trailer they call "The God Mobile." The back of the trailer becomes a table for them to put literature on. Above the trailer is a large sign that reads, "Are you going to heaven? Two Question Test Reveals Answer." Local churches are invited to supply personnel to man the booth. In the past ten years, they have led over 32,208 people in a salvation prayer.

As people pass by the booth, the workers invite people to take the spiritual test. The God Mobile uses a flip-book with this test as a tool for people to do the spiritual survey.

Page 1:
Are you going to heaven? Two Question Test Reveals Answer

Page 2:
Question #1 Do you believe that you will go to heaven when you die?
>   1. Yes
>   2. I Hope So
>   3. No
>   4. I'm Not Sure

Page 3:
Question #2 Why do you believe this?
>   1. I keep the 10 Commandments
>   2. I go to church.
>   3. I believe in God.
>   4. I am a good person.
>   5. I have done the best I can.

6. I never hurt anyone.

7. _____ is my Savior.

Page 4:

According to the Bible the answers 1-6 on the previous page will not get you into heaven. Your good works of religion are not enough to get you into heaven (Titus 3:3).

Can I quickly share with you the only way the Bible describes how someone can get into heaven?

Page 5:

The PROBLEM. The Bible says...the wages of sin is death (eternal separation from God's presence) Rom 6:23

Your sin has separated your from God! (Isaiah 59:2).

In light of this problem...God supplied the solution for you.

Page 6:

The SOLUTION Because God loved us all so much, He devised a plan that placed the death penalty for sin upon the only person in the universe who could take away our sin, the Lord Jesus Christ, the Son of God. (Heb. 2:9; John 3:19).

Though Jesus didn't deserve it, He suffered and died on the cross in our place, providing the only way from mankind to have eternal life and go to heaven (John 17:3).

Jesus' death and resurrection enables us to be forgiven of our sins and gives us the power to no longer be controlled by sin (John 3:8).

Page 7:

Conclusion To Receive Jesus as your Savior you must...

* Be sorry for your sin and ask God to forgive you of your sin.
* Be willing to turn away from your sin.
* Have faith in what Jesus did for you on the cross to forgive your sin.

When you turn from your sin and trust in Jesus, there will be a supernatural change in your heart which the Bible calls being "born-again" (spiritually, not physically) The Holy Spirit comes when you confess Jesus as your Savior, so you can be "born-again" (John 3:3).

Page 8:

The Bible says "...that if you confess with your mouth that Jesus is Lord and believe in your heart that God has raised Him from the dead, you will be saved" (Romans 10:9).

So, you can go to heaven and receive eternal life with Jesus as your Savior by sincerely confessing the following prayer. (Please pray loud enough to hear with your own voice.)

Page 9:

The Salvation Prayer

"Lord Jesus, I believe that you died on the cross for my sins and rose from the dead. I know I'm a sinner and I ask you to forgive me of my sins. I repent now, and turn away from sin. I receive you, Jesus, as my personal Savior. I ask you to fill me with your Holy Spirit. Thank you Jesus for Your love, the gift of eternal life, and the kingdom of heaven. Amen."

Page 10:

Now that you are going to heaven, Welcome to the family of God.
* Being a Christian is having a personal relationship with God.

* Pray and read God's Word daily so you will grow as a Christian. (Begin with the Gospel of John)
* Join a Bible teaching church where you can worship and be baptized.
* Build new relationships with other believers.
* Share your faith with others as God gives you opportunity.

Page 11:
Now you are heaven bound, Congratulations! Today is your spiritual birthday.

Here is some advice from the God Mobile Handbook concerning giving the test:

* Do not touch any prospective test-taker; it may be viewed by the authorities as harassment.
* Do NOT shout at people to take the test. As they pass the booth, politely ask them to take the spiritual test. The suggested invitation is: "Would you like to take our two-question test?" or "Would you like to take our test? It is free."
* It is not the position of the ministry to argue with anyone over doctrine or religions. Workers will spot the argumentative types very quickly because they will not accept what you have to say or after you have answered one question, they will shoot another question at you. If the worker senses the purpose of the argumentative person, look them straight in the eye and firmly tell them, "Our reason to be here is to show you how to get to heaven." End the conversation then and there. Such argumentative encounters are futile and lead to nothing. The arguers will only get louder and more disruptive. Passersby may get an unfavorable impression of the ministry, if the argument is not terminated immediately.

Section 8:
Reach Communities in Your Community

Outreach Idea #133: Coffee House. One church in South Dakota started a coffee house near a local college campus. They provided comfortable seating, inexpensive coffee, and free Internet access. Students came in to study and the church used the opportunity to develop relationships and to start conversations about God. Regular Bible studies are held for those interested.

The people who gather in coffee houses usually have time on their hands to talk and to listen. Value each person who comes in, get to know them and their background. As you develop genuine relationships, you will have opportunities to share the Gospel.

Outreach Idea #134: Concert. Invite a popular music group to your church. Many people will come to hear music that would not come to hear a sermon.

Indonesia is the largest Muslim nation in the world. Many evangelists who have tried to hold "crusades" in Indonesia have been run out of town. We decided to do a concert instead of a crusade. We invited local music groups to come perform. One of the finalists from "Indonesian Idol" was our guest star. He was a believer in Jesus in

the midst of a Muslim nation. In between the various secular acts we did dramas and shared testimonies about Jesus. At one of our concerts, over 8,000 young Muslims heard the Gospel for the first time. Watch On-Line:http://www.youtube.com/watch?v=x9gejx-sX50

Outreach Idea #135: Mobile-Kids Clubs (AKA: Sidewalk Sunday School). Amber Baker is the director of the Mobile-Kids Clubs at Victory Christian Center in Tulsa, Oklahoma. The church owns several bread trucks that have been converted into outreach tools. The trucks are painted in bright orange and lime and a sound system is mounted on the roof. The side of each truck folds down to become a platform. Volunteers fill the truck with groceries and travel to a low-income housing complex. When the truck arrives, the music is cranked up and kids come running. Games, songs, memory verses, prizes, and illustrated sermons are used to communicate the Gospel. Afterwards, every adult receives a bag of free groceries.

Outreach Idea #136: Minster to Athletes. Pastor John Adams at New Life Church in Huron, Ohio, is a fanatical triathlon competitor who loves ministering to other athletes. He started training for triathlons at the age of 55. His ministry puts up a booth at races to give out water and to pray with people. At many races, he volunteers to be a "last place finisher." He runs right behind the slowest triathlete so they do not have to be the last person to cross the finish line. His encouragement is often what it takes to get people to complete the race.

Outreach Idea #137: Start a Spanish Service. Tom Brown of Word of Life in El Paso, Texas, realized that many people in his community speak Spanish. He decided to start a Spanish service at his church. He hired a Spanish-speaking pastor and started to advertise the service in local newspapers. Every Sunday afternoon, as soon as the English service is finished, the Spanish service started in

the same auditorium. Within just a few months, the Spanish service at Word of Life had over 120 people attending.

Outreach Idea #138: Prison Ministry. Steve Young runs Victory Bible Institute in over one hundred prisons across the American Midwest. He was incarcerated himself, and, after he became a Christian, he started reaching out to men and women in jail. The benefit to preaching in prison is that you have a captive audience! Prison, for many, is the lowest point of their lives, and inmates often start asking questions about purpose and meaning in life. Many are willing to turn to God for help. Most prisons have chaplains who are looking for volunteers to help minister. In order to minister on a regular basis in a prison you have to go through a background check and get a special ID.

John Green describes the process of being approved to work in prisons in Oklahoma. He writes, "I have been a volunteer through the Prison Invasion ministry for almost 2 years. The prison volunteer ministry is vital to the rehabilitation of those who seek help and desire to grow in a relationship with the Lord. I have enjoyed the relationships that I have formed and the opportunity to share the gospel with those of other ethnicities, religions, and spiritual backgrounds. One of the best feelings in the world is to lead someone who is lost to Christ.

"1. In order to get started in prison ministry you must first submit a volunteer application to the Department of Corrections (DOC). They will forward your application to the FBI to conduct an extensive background check. They will often require that you send in three recommendations along with your application.

"2. Once you pass the background check, you will be notified by the DOC as to when the next orientation meeting will be held and what

you are required to bring to that orientation. The required items are two forms of identification. Orientation usually lasts about 8 hours. Once orientation is complete, your picture will be taken for the passes required to enter into a DOC facility. You will receive two badges. One badge you will need to wear at all times while visiting a facility and the other will remain at the guards desk so that they know who is still inside the prison in case of an emergency.

3. Find a place where you would like to minister/volunteer –whether it be the City Jail, a Minimum Security Prison, a Medium Security Prison, or a Maximum Security Prison. In order to get access into the facility you will need to meet with the chaplain of the facility in which you plan to volunteer. Most likely there are other groups that are already volunteering and you will discuss what kind of volunteering it is that you would like to do (whether it is a church service, Bible study classes, or one-on-one ministry for example). The chaplain will let you know what you can and cannot do while at the prison and also what times you can enter.

4. Finally, start volunteering! I volunteer at 3 different facilities here in Oklahoma. I go to Vinita, known as the Northeastern Oklahoma Correctional Center, every 1st Saturday of the month. We usually start around 1 pm and minister in the facilities in a one-on-one capacity until 4 pm. While inside, we visit with the inmates where they live and minister to them on the yard. We are also able to go into their recreational areas where they play pool, dominoes, and chess. We break for dinner, and return to the facility at 6 pm for a service that lasts till about 8 pm. During this time we sing songs and enjoy praise and worship. We give the inmates an opportunity to share their personal testimonies and a message is preached. We often go with the thought that we are taking the Word to them, but, most of the time, it is us who are inspired to live life even better. We watch people grow spiritually, and it truly is a blessing to see those men be

on fire for the Lord.

"The next facility that I visit is the Eddie Warrior Correctional Center in Taft. This is a minimum-security prison. We go into this facility on the first Thursday of every month and we join them with a worship service that includes songs, testimonials and preaching. This is an all-women facility and we do not do one-on-one counseling there. However, there are groups that come during the week to have Bible studies. These women are hungry for the Lord and look forward to each of our visits.

"The last ministry opportunity is every third Saturday of the month when we go to the Dick Conner Correctional facility, located in Hominy, Oklahoma. This is a medium security facility. We volunteer from 9:00 a.m. to 1:00 p.m. here. In this facility, the units are grouped in two's with their own separate recreational facilities in order to keep the violence between gangs to a minimum. They also have a unit that is 'faith based.' In this unit you have people who are in Bible correspondence courses, attending various schools, working on college degrees, and trying to improve themselves. We alternate units that we visit and try to establish relationships between mature believers and those who have recently accepted the Lord.

"These are just a few examples of evangelism behind the walls of a prison. There are often different programs already operating in prisons that you can join, or you can set up a program that best fits your schedule. All you need is a heart for Christ and a willingness to serve."

Outreach Idea #139: Reach Out to Local Schools.
1. Ask if you can lead a prayer during the General Assembly.
2. Share at your school's Career Day about your vocation as a minister.

3. Help the children and teachers at a local school start a Bible Club.
4. Encourage the young people in your church to talk to their friends about God.

Outreach Idea #140: Public School Assembly. Evangelist John Smithwick hosts E3 youth events. During the day, his team does an anti-drug, anti-alcohol, and anti-violence assembly in public schools and at night he does an evangelism service.

Brandon Querin, an intern with John's ministry, explains that during the day events at the public school, John discusses how the negative forces of this world can bring you down and cause you to not rise to your full potential. During the assembly, the E3 team will perform skits and dramas that show the importance of making good decisions. They show a video presentation of a young high school football player who has everything going for him until he loses it all due to a drunk-driving accident. After the video presentation, John comes back on the stage to encourage students to commit to living drug and alcohol-free by standing up and repeating an oath of right living. At the end of the assembly, the students are invited back to attend a night event that includes a concert and a prize giveaway (a flat screen TV or an Xbox 360).

In the evening, a local band starts the night event with a concert that covers secular music. Then the ministry team does drama presentations that show the spiritual side of life and how there is a constant war going on between God and the devil for souls. After the drama, John tells the young people that committing to live a life free from negative forces is not enough, that people also need help to stand against sin, and that that is why Jesus died on the cross. All the students are then given the opportunity to receive Christ as Savior.

Outreach Idea #141: Skate Park Shakedown. Joshua Hurd shares

that in Mannford, Oklahoma there is a skate park that is open to the community. With permission from the city council, his church hosts a skateboarding contest for a grand prize of a professional-grade skateboard and a $100 gift certificate. Entertainment includes the city's best young skateboarders, live music, a DJ, and free cheeseburgers. After the contest, Joshua preaches and gives an altar call.

Outreach Idea #142: Apologetics Conference. Pastor Jim Burkett from Southwood Baptist Church in Tulsa, Oklahoma, frequently does this type of event. He calls it "Apologetics on Fire." Many people in our society are skeptics and unbelievers. We must engage these people on an intellectual level if we are to lead them to Jesus. The primary target group of this conference is high school and college age students. Perhaps a debate could be arranged with an atheist?

Possible questions to address at this conference include:
Is evolution true or did God create the world?
Is the Bible a book of fairy tales?
Can morality exist without God?
Why do bad things happen to good people?

Outreach Idea #143: Question and Answer Night. Encourage the local community to come to the church and ask any question they have about Christianity. Many people in our world feel that the church only offers a monologue and not a dialogue. They do not want to be preached at, but they do have genuine questions about spiritual issues. Advertise a special night when people can come and ask the pastor any question they want to ask.

Outreach Idea #144: Monday Night Football. Robert Hogrefe loves football. He suggests inviting guys to your house to watch the big game. Over time, as you develop relationships you will be able

to share the Gospel. Do not "beat them over the head" with Jesus at the start. Slowly turn the conversation over the course of a few weeks towards Jesus. Once your friends are saved, use them to help invite other unsaved friends to watch the pigskin fly.

Outreach Idea #145: Backyard Bible Club. Invite the children in your community to come over to your house once a week. Many parents might leap at the opportunity for a free baby sitter. Play Bible-oriented games and sing songs with the children. Use puppets or clowns to share about God.

Outreach Idea #146: Cross-Cultural Celebration. Promote diversity by inviting another cultural group to bring ethnic dishes or presentations to your church. For example, visit the local mosque in your community and ask the imam to bring his people to your church. Give him the opportunity to do a short presentation about Islam and then you do a short presentation about Jesus. In order to reach a Muslim, you must first become a friend, only then will he be willing to listen to you.

Outreach Idea #147: Ladies' Weekend Shopping Trip. Julie Scott writes, "Ladies love to get together and shop. This is a great event for the ladies in your church to invite their friends and family to. A shopping trip to the nearest outlet mall is a relaxed environment where any woman would be comfortable to join their "church-going" friend. Throw in some great ministry in the midst of the shopping trip and the ladies will quickly see that your church is a place where they can fit in and feel at home. There are many women who have never attended church or had a negative church experience when they were younger. With an event like a weekend shopping trip, they can be introduced to the ladies of your church outside of the church building and actually build relationships with those ladies. Then, they will have more courage to actually darken the door

the church for a weekend service.

Here are some tips for planning a Ladies' Weekend Shopping Trip:

* Promote the Shopping Trip as an outreach. The ladies in your church can invite their neighbors, co-workers, and sisters. Be sure that it's not just a shopping day for the women that are already active in church, but really get them involved in recruiting their unchurched friends and family members.

* Sell tickets. You do not want to sell tickets for a profit, but to cover expenses such as gas money and hotel reservations. Also, you will get your church ladies' more involved if they buy a ticket for a friend to give away. If a lady sees that a ticket has been bought for her, she will feel special and will make a point to put it on her calendar to attend.

* Put together an itinerary to distribute. You will want to be sure that the ladies are aware of everything that the weekend shopping trip has to offer. Include the names of the stores that you will be visiting, special prizes that will be given, etc. You will want to include some special activities such as a late-night party after the first shopping day and a morning devotional breakfast to provide some ministry time.

* You can take church vans/buses or rent a nice coach bus (depending on your budget). Be sure each vehicle has at least one leader from your church to help with organizing the ladies, answering their questions, and promoting fellowship along the way.

* Meet with the office of the outlet mall or the merchant association if you're going to a shopping district. Organize as much as you can with these people in advance of the shopping trip. For example, lo-

cate where the vans/buses are authorized to park. Get coupon booklets and flyers with special deals to give to your group. Some stores will be very excited about your group and will even hang welcome signs and have draws especially for your ladies.

* Negotiate a special group price at the local hotel so that you're not paying full price.

* Organize the ladies rooming arrangements for sharing rooms.

* Have a late-night party when all the ladies get together and have fun. Reserve a banquet room/meeting room at the hotel for this. Plan mixer games, door prizes, karaoke, board games, and snacks. This is a great way for the ladies to make new friends.

* The next morning, have a breakfast devotional time. This would be in the same banquet room/meeting room in the hotel. Depending on the hotel, you could have a breakfast buffet or something catered. This is where the ministry happens. At this point in the trip, they've had fun and built new relationships, and now they are more receptive to hearing what you have to say. You can do a simple time of worship and a brief message. This is a great opportunity to minister to the women and show them that your church is a place that they would enjoy coming every week."

Outreach Ideas #148: Fun Trip. Sponsor an activity that is easy for your members to invite unsaved family, friends, co-workers, and others to participate in. The goal should be to have 50% church members go and 50% people that need Jesus. Examples of activities are:
* Ski Trip
* Golf Outing
* Fishing

95

* Camping
* Hunting
* Road Trip

The point of the trip is to build relationships outside of the church with people who need to make their way into the church.

Outreach Idea #149: Themed Sunday. Once each month do a themed Sunday outreach that is easy for your members to invite their friends to. Here are some ideas:
* Sandwich Sunday - Make the world's longest sub.
* Ice Cream Sunday - Give away ice cream cones.
* Chili Cook-off Sunday - Have a contest and give a prize for the best chili.
* Hot Dog Sunday - Fire up the grills and give away hotdogs.
* Pot Luck Sunday - This has been done for as long as believers can remember.
* International Sunday - Serve food from different countries.
* Sports Sunday – Ask everyone to wear a jersey from their favorite team. Invite players from a local team to come sign autographs.

Outreach Idea #150: Days of Honor. Who can you honor in your community? Pick a group of community heroes to honor and then invite representatives from that group to come to your church. Spend some time in your Sunday morning service to thank these people.
* First Responder's Appreciation Day – Honor firemen, policemen, and ambulance drivers. Invite the firemen to park their trucks right in front of the church with their ladders in the air and lights flashing.
* Teacher's Appreciation Day – Ask every child in the church to invite his or her teacher to come receive a certificate of appreciation.
* Public Servant's Appreciation Day - Invite your mayor, the city board, and the school board to come visit your church.
* Farmer's Appreciation Day

* Trash Collector's Appreciation Day
* Military Appreciation Day – Honor those who have helped to protect our country.
* Medical Professional Appreciation Day

Every time you do an "Appreciation Day," make sure you call your local media to come take pictures. This is the type of feel-good story they are looking for. Not only will these outreaches give you an excuse to invite new people into your church, but you will also build up a reservoir of good will in your community.

Outreach Idea #151: Children's Day. Sunday Ololade says that May 27 is Children's Day in Nigeria. He suggests doing a special outreach to celebrate the children in your community. His church does a party for the kids and gives each child a shirt that says, "We are the future." He says many Muslim families in Nigeria have been reached because they see how the Christians care for the children.

Outreach Idea #152: Wedding Planning Offer wedding planning to couples in your community, especially to those who are already living together. Provide pre-marital counseling, church venue, wedding décor, and assistance with bulletins and invitations. Your church could offer this as a wedding package to non-members specifically to those with low income.

Section 9:
The Main Idea

Outreach Idea #153: Love People. The final and greatest way to reach people is by loving them. People do not care how much you know, until they know how much you care. Here is a modern day translation of 1 Corinthians 13 for the evangelistic pastor.

If I preach like a mighty preacher with great eloquence and fire, and have not love, I am but a clanging symbol.

Though I use my talents to do impressive feats that fill up auditoriums and have not love, then I am nothing.

Even if I sing like the angels and record best-selling Christian songs, and have not love, then I am like fingernails pulled across a chalkboard.

And though I share all my belongings and feed the hungry, and have not love, then I am hollow.

If thousands of people stream forward at my altar calls and people flood into the doors of my church building, and I have not love, then I have accomplished nothing.

Regardless of how many tracts I give away or people I invite to my home group, if I have not love, I have missed the point.

Love suffers long and is kind; love does not envy; love does not parade itself, is not puffed up; does not behave rudely, does not seek its own, is not provoked, thinks no evil; does not rejoice in iniquity, but rejoices in the truth; bears all things, believes all things, hopes all things, endures all things.

Love never fails. But whether there are amazing evangelism techniques, they will fail; whether there are visitors who come to church every Sunday, they will cease; whether there is knowledge about how to reach a post-modern culture, it will vanish away.

And now abide three tools for the evangelistic church; faith, hope, love, these three; but the greatest of these is love.

Conclusion

The Apostle spoke of "becoming all things to all people so that by all possible means" some might be saved. While this book may not contain the comprehensive list, the "all possible means" of reaching out to people, I have tried to outline as many ways as I could think of as means for you to reach out to your community—things that others have done, things that I have done myself, things that have worked with large and small churches, in churches in America and around the world, with the young and with the old. We have Good News to share, and we need to be active and creative in the ways that we go about sharing it, so that the goal of seeing lost people find their way home to God can be accomplished.

My hope and prayer, as you have read this book, is that your heart will be stirred for the lost and that your hands will be strengthened to reach out to them.

What is Your Best Outreach Idea?

I want to hear from you!

* What is your church doing to reach out to the lost?
* What methods have you found to be effective for evangelism?
* Is there a needy community near your church that you have adopted?
* What church growth methods have worked for you?
* Do you have any testimonies of people who have been saved in your outreaches?
* Do you have any ideas for improving the outreaches listed in this book?

Tell me what God has done in your church as you have taken steps to impact your community, and I will feature your story on my blog and put your ideas in the next edition of this book. How have you reached out to your community?

_____

_____

_____

_____

_____

_____

_____

_____

_____

_____

_____

_____

_____

_____

_____

_____

_____

_____

_____

_____

_____

_____

_____

_____

_____

_____

_____

_____

_____

_____

_____

_____

_____

Mail Your Outreach Idea To:

Daniel King
PO Box 701113
Tulsa, OK 74170
or e-mail: daniel@kingministries.com

Our Goal?
Every Soul!

Daniel & Jessica King

About the Author

Daniel King and his wife Jessica met in the middle of Africa while they were both on a mission trip. They are in high demand as speakers at churches and conferences all over North America. Their passion, energy, and enthusiasm are enjoyed by audiences everywhere they go.

They are international missionary evangelists who do massive soul-winning festivals in countries around the world. Their passion for the lost has taken them to over sixty nations preaching the gospel to crowds that often exceed 50,000 people.

Daniel was called into the ministry when he was five years old and began to preach when he was six. His parents became missionaries to Mexico when he was ten. When he was fourteen he started a children's ministry that gave him the opportunity to minister in some of America's largest churches while still a teenager.

At the age of fifteen, Daniel read a book where the author encouraged young people to set a goal to earn $1,000,000. Daniel reinterpreted the message and determined to win 1,000,000 people to Christ every year.

Daniel has authored ten books including his best sellers *Grace Wins*, *Healing Power*, *The Secret of Obed-Edom*, and *Fire Power*. His book *Welcome to the Kingdom* has been given away to tens of thousands of new believers.

Soul Winning Festivals

Metu, Ethiopia

Khushpur, Pakistan

Roca Blanca, Mexico

Sialkot, Pakistan

Agere Maryam, Ethiopia

Kisaran, Indonesia

THE Million Heirs Club

When Daniel King was fifteen years old, he set a goal to lead 1,000,000 people to Jesus before his 30th birthday. Instead of trying to become a millionaire, he decided to lead a million "heirs" into the kingdom of God. *"If you belong to Christ then you are heirs"* (Galatians 3:29).

After celebrating the completion of this goal, Daniel & Jessica made it their mission to go for one million souls every year.

This **Quest for Souls** is accomplished through:
* Soul Winning Festivals
* Leadership Training
* Literature Distribution
* Humanitarian Relief

Would you help us lead
people to Jesus by joining
The MillionHeir's Club?

Visit www.kingministries.com to get involved!

MASTER SOUL WINNER

Information on how to reach the lost. Learn practical tips on sharing your faith with friends and family.

$10.00

SOUL WINNING

Inspiration for reaching the lost. Do you have a passion for the lost? This book shares over 150 truths about soul winning.

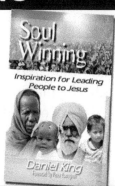

$10.00

CALL OF THE SOUL WINNER

Motivation for reaching the lost. This book amplifies three voices that are calling for you to be a soul winner.

$10.00

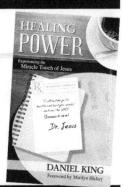

WRITE A BOOK

* Why you should write a book.
* How to put your ideas on paper.
* Ways to overcome writer's block.
* Secrets of Editing, Designing, Publishing, and Marketing Your Book.

$12.00

RAISING MONEY

* 10 Secrets of Raising Money for your Ministry.
* How to finance the vision God has given you.
* Why it is more important to be a "friend-raiser than a "fund-raiser."

$12.00

BOOKING SPEAKING ENGAGEMENTS

For the last ten years, Daniel King has ministered an average of one hundred times every year in North America. In this short but explosive book written for traveling ministers he shares the secrets that will help you succeed in the traveling ministry!

$12.00

The vision of King Ministries is to lead 1,000,000 people to Jesus every year and to train believers to become leaders.

To contact Daniel & Jessica King:

Write:
King Ministries International
PO Box 701113
Tulsa, OK 74170 USA

King Ministries Canada
PO Box 3401
Morinville, Alberta T8R 1S3 Canada

Call toll-free:
1-877-431-4276

Visit us online:
www.kingministries.com

E-Mail:
daniel@kingministries.com

CPSIA information can be obtained
at www.ICGtesting.com
Printed in the USA
BVHW050721201218
536072BV00014B/637/P